NEIL T. ANDERSON & TOM C. McGEE, JR.

HELPING OTHERS FIND

FREEDOM IN CHRIST

Training Manual & Study Guide

Gospel Light

PUBLISHING STAFF
Jean Daly, Managing Editor
Pam Weston, Editorial Assistant
Kyle Duncan, Editorial Director
Bayard Taylor, M. Div., Editor, Theological and Biblical Issues
Mario Ricketts, Designer
Lisa Guest, Contributing Editor

ISBN 0-8307-1759-5
© 1995 Neil T. Anderson and Tom C. McGee, Jr.
All rights reserved.
Printed in U.S.A.

CONTENTS

ACKNOWLEDGMENTS

As this ministry of helping people find freedom in Christ has spread throughout the world, we have learned valuable lessons from every counseling session we've had, every conference we've done, and every culture of every country we've visited. We are, however, especially indebted to Freedom Ministries, a joint venture of Crystal Evangelical Free Church in Hope, Minnesota, and Student Venture in the Twin Cities.

Freedom Ministries was formed after I (Neil) conducted my "Resolving Personal and Spiritual Conflicts" conference in April 1993. Through the faithful leadership of John Sather, Irv Woolf, Carolyn Fugate, Shelly Olson and many others, this one ministry has guided nearly a thousand people to freedom in Christ, and the vast majority of the counseling was done by trained laypeople. Since that spring, Freedom Ministries has networked with many other churches in the Twin Cities area to provide training for other lay encouragers. And these lay counselors are a shining example of what this book is all about. In fact, they pioneered some of the terminology, forms and training ideas for developing a freedom ministry that you'll find here.

We are indebted to Freedom Ministries and to every individual and every church that has invited us to be a part of their lives. What we have learned from those experiences we now pass on to you. We believe that every church in the world can and should be able to establish their people free in Christ. To that end we dedicate this book.

Neil T. Anderson
Tom C. McGee, Jr.

ESTABLISHING A FREEDOM MINISTRY

MINISTERING IN TRUTH, UNITY AND LOVE: AN INTRODUCTION

Have you ever wondered why we Christians aren't living more fruitful lives and why so many of us are falling into immorality? Scripture clearly offers us the assurance of victory—"In all these things we overwhelmingly conquer through Him who loved us" (Romans 8:37); "I can do all things through Him who strengthens me" (Philippians 4:13); and "Now those who belong to Christ Jesus have crucified the flesh with its passions and desires" (Galatians 5:24), to quote just a few. And aren't you just a little tired of attending how-to seminars that either teach you how to improve your acting ability ("You can be a victorious believer!") or scold you for not having more faith or doing better as a Christian? Certainly just trying harder can't be the answer to finding freedom from the struggle which many of us believers face or from the sin which we can't seem to escape. So what is?

Is Jesus Christ the answer? Does God's truth—revealed in the Bible, His written Word, and His Son, the Living Word—really set us free? We have never been more convinced that the answer to both these questions is emphatically "Yes!" But the track record of most churches seems to suggest otherwise. Case in point: I (Neil) conducted a conference in a church where the three previous pastors had all left because of sexual immorality. This kind of failure on the part of Christian leaders makes it even more difficult for believers in the pews to believe they truly can find victory and freedom in Christ.

The Lord's perspective on immorality and bondage among believers could be very helpful, and the apostle John affords us the opportunity to hear His perspective in John 17, a passage known as the High Priestly Prayer. Facing death, Jesus is about to return to the Father and leave behind His disciples (Judas has already betrayed Christ). At this point, Jesus commissions these faithful eleven to go into a less-than-receptive world and make disciples. As He does so—and this is important for us to note—Jesus identifies Satan as the ruler of this world (see John 16:11).

And this truth is echoed throughout the New Testament by Jesus' closest followers. In his first epistle, John writes, "the whole world lies in the power of the evil one" (1 John 5:19). Likewise, Paul says, "the god of this world has blinded the minds of the unbelieving" (2 Corinthians 4:4) and admonishes us to put on the armor of God "for our struggle is not against flesh and blood, but against the rulers, against the powers, against the world forces of this darkness, against the spiritual forces of wickedness in the heavenly places" (Ephesians 6:12). Peter adds his voice with, "Be of sober spirit, be on the alert. Your adversary, the devil, prowls about like a roaring lion, seeking someone to devour" (1 Peter 5:8). These verses are not optional passages. We cannot dismiss them as though there is no such thing as a spiritual world or kingdom of darkness. In the face of this reality, Jesus prays, "I do not ask Thee to take [My disciples] out of the world, but to keep them from the evil one. They are not of the world, even as I am not of the world. Sanctify them in the truth; Thy word is truth" (John 17:15-17). In this verse lies the first of three keys to establishing a freedom ministry for believers.

MINISTRY IN TRUTH

As pastors, we have dealt with many people whom we knew had spiritual problems—but we didn't have any idea how to help them. Seminary had not prepared us to confront the reality of the spiritual world, nor did we know of any effective tools for doing so. We didn't even have a clear understanding of who we were as children of God or why such an understanding is necessary to knowing freedom in Christ. After all, our own identity was wrapped up in what we were doing as pastors!

I (Tom) had taken courses in Christian counseling, read just about every book in the field, sponsored seminars, and relentlessly taught people about the grace of God. Yet there were many dear—and sometimes desperate—Christians who seemingly could not connect with God. They had no idea who they were in Christ—and looking back, I'm not sure I knew who I was in Christ either.

Soon after I (Neil) joined the faculty at Talbot School of Theology, I developed and offered a graduate class on spiritual warfare. At first, the course was a classic example of the blind leading the blind. I felt like a first-grader teaching kindergarten students. But as the class size doubled every year, I started to see some tremendous things happen in the lives of the students. Spiritual warfare is a reality, and believers are hungry to know what to do to find the victory Christ offers them.

In the last few years, we have had the privilege of personally counseling hundreds of people who were struggling with their thought lives, experiencing difficulty reading their Bibles, or actually hearing voices in their heads. With very few exceptions, their problem was a spiritual battle for their minds. Paul writes in 1 Timothy 4:1(*NIV*), "The Spirit clearly says that in later times some will abandon the faith and follow deceiving spirits and things taught by demons"—and that's exactly what is happening all over the world today. It is happening in your church and in the lives of believers you know.

What are these lost and deceived, these hurting and captive people to do? We have learned how to help such people find their freedom in Christ. In addition, thousands of other people have found their freedom in Christ when, in our conferences, we walk them through the Steps to Freedom, a process now being taught all over the world in many different languages.

The key to this process was my (Neil's) realization that what we were dealing with is best described as a "truth encounter," not just a "power encounter." After all, it is truth—God's truth—that sets us free (see John 8:32). Since the battle we are dealing with is primarily for our minds, we need to take every thought captive in obedience to Christ (see 2 Corinthians 10:5) and think upon that which is true (see Philippians 4:8). This battle for our minds is certainly not a new phenomenon: Eve was deceived; she believed a lie. Paul acknowledges this fact when he writes, "I am afraid, lest as the serpent deceived Eve by his craftiness, your minds should be led astray from the simplicity and purity of devotion to Christ" (2 Corinthians 11:3). The Early Church father Irenaeus nailed the problem when he wrote, "The devil, however, as he is the apostate angel, can only go to this length, as he did at the beginning, to deceive and lead astray the mind of man into disobeying the commandments of God, and gradually to darken the hearts."

Concern that His people would be deceived motivated God to intervene dramatically in the Early Church when He struck down Ananias and Sapphira (see Acts 5). Their sin was keeping for themselves half the amount they had received from the sale of their land but allowing people to think they had given the full price. Most people wouldn't consider that a capital offense. After all, it was just their own cunning idea—or was it? Notice what Scripture says: "Ananias, why has Satan filled your heart to lie to the Holy Spirit?" (Acts 5:3). The Lord knew that the primary battle was for the mind so He sent an early message about the importance of honesty and integrity among His people.

Jesus echoes His Father's concern for truth in the High Priestly Prayer when He prays, "Keep them from the evil one.... Sanctify them in the truth; Thy word is truth" (John 17:15,17). Many believers today who struggle in their Christian walk incorrectly reason that what they lack is power. Consequently, they often look for some new experience that will give them more power. This approach leads only to disaster, for not one verse in the Bible instructs us to seek power. We already have all the power we need to live the Christian life. That is why Paul prays "that the eyes of your heart may be enlightened, so that you may know what is the hope of His calling, what are the riches of the glory of His inheritance in the saints and what is the surpassing greatness of His power toward us who believe" (Ephesians 1:18,19).

In a tragically similar fashion, many struggling Christians are desperately trying to become someone they already are. Few Christians know who they are as children of God, nor do they understand their inheritance in Christ or, as mentioned above, know the power they already have as believers. In fact, none of the people that I (Neil) was trying to help in the early days of developing this ministry knew their identity as children of God or the significance of that identity. They needed to know the truth that Paul writes in Galatians 4:6: "Because you are sons, God has sent forth the Spirit of His Son into our hearts, crying 'Abba! Father'"— and the ramifications of this truth for them personally.

Why don't we Christians know and understand our identity in Christ? Why isn't this biblical truth a powerful factor in the life of every believer? After all, Scripture teaches, "The Spirit himself bears witness with our spirit that we are children of God" (Romans 8:16). The apostle John teaches, "As many as received Him, to them He gave the right to become children of God" (John 1:12) and, in 1 John 3:1, he writes, "See how great a love the Father has bestowed upon us, that we should be called children of God; and such we are."

Why have we believers not understood this truth? Some credit can be given to the evil one, the deceiver, the father of lies. Many believers ignore the reality of his existence and overlook the reality of the spiritual world. The study of spiritual conflicts has little academic credibility in higher education because of our materialistic western worldview. (One leading educator wouldn't list a class on resolving spiritual conflicts because he feared the school would lose accreditation!) Furthermore, society would have us believe that there is a natural explanation for everything and therefore a natural answer for everything. That perspective is simply not true. If it were, the gospel would be meaningless in this present life.

Some believers boldly proclaim, "I can't have a spiritual problem because I'm a Christian!" Incredible! Is the armor of God (see Ephesians 6:11-17) for the non-Christian? We can and will indeed have problems in this world. Jesus promises as much in John 16:33 and, aware of these inevitable struggles, asks God in John 17 to protect believers and help them stand strong in their faith. When we deny our problems—spiritual and otherwise—and attempt to cover them up, we play right into the hands of the deceiver.

Too many Christians have abdicated responsibility for helping struggling believers, referring them to secular therapists who rely heavily on drug therapy, human wisdom and self-help programs rather than on God's eternal truth. Although we thank God for medical doctors and we do believe in the appropriate use of medication, we also believe that much of what is being labeled "mental illness" may actually be a spiritual battle for the mind. Our society's natural worldview leads us to believe that any problem taking place between our ears is primarily a hardware problem. We disagree. We think it is primarily a software problem. Like computers, our minds must be programmed right or we won't function right. It is therefore not a surprise that one of the primary calls of the New Testament is to renew our minds (see Romans 12:2) and then live by faith according to what God says is true.

Clearly, our churches need to step forward with God's truth and His prescription for freedom from sinful and defeated lives. The Steps to Freedom in Christ provides churches with a plan that will enable them to take a bold stand for God's truth and show people that His truth is indeed what will set them free (see John 8:32,36). People around the world are finding resolution to personal and spiritual conflicts that are keeping them in bondage: they are finding spiritual freedom in Christ.

MINISTRY IN UNITY

Having asked that His disciples be "sanctified in truth" (John 17:19), Jesus continues the High Priestly Prayer with the petition that "they may all be one; even as Thou, Father, art in Me, and I in Thee, that they may be in Us; that the world may believe that Thou didst send Me" (v. 21). It must grieve the Lord to see the churches in America divided into theological camps, denominational distinctives, and various sectarian groups. The Body of Christ is not dwelling together in unity.

The basis for unity is not our common physical heritage, our religious traditions, or even our shared theology. Now don't get us wrong—we are totally committed to the Word of God, which is the truth. Theology, however, is our attempt to systematize truth. None of us fallible, finite humans can or should claim that our theological perspective is perfectly right. The only One who is right is God. His Word never changes even as we have continued to refine and teach a systematic theology.

The basis for unity among believers lies therefore not in our common physical heritage, traditions or theological distinctives. Instead, unity among believers lies in our common spiritual heritage: every born-again Christian is a child of God. Paul urges every one of us born-again Christians "to walk in a manner worthy of the calling with which you have been called, with all humility and gentleness, with patience, showing forbearance to one another in love, being diligent to preserve the unity of the Spirit in the bond of peace" (Ephesians 4:1-3).

We need to have a healthy tolerance of other Christian perspectives and celebrate what we have in common. We believe this is starting to happen in America, that Jesus' prayer in John 17:23— "I in them, and Thou in Me, that they may be perfected in unity"—is being answered. Ministries like Promise Keepers, March for Jesus, prayer summits, and others are uniting previously diverse groups. Only if our identity is found in Christ can such bridges be built and unity achieved. Again, we come back to the importance of knowing who we are as children of God.

As we've noted, one reason we don't know who we are as children of God is because we are being deceived about our identity by the father of lies. Let us also offer two other possible explanations. First, we are too often laboring under half a gospel. We know Jesus as the Messiah who died for our sins; we know that, if we will believe in Him, our sins will be forgiven and when we die we will get to go to heaven. Presenting the gospel this way, however, can give the impression that eternal life is something we get when we die. Not true! We are alive in Christ right now: "He who has the Son has the life; he who does not have the Son of God does not have the life" (1 John 5:12).

According to Ephesians 2:1, we were all born dead in our trespasses and sins. In other words, we were born physically alive, but spiritually dead. Now, if you wanted to save a dead man, what would you do? Give him life? If that were all you did, he would only die again. First, you would have to cure the disease that caused him to die. The Bible clearly teaches that the disease which caused our spiritual death is sin. Paul writes, "The wages of sin is death" (Romans 6:23). So Jesus went to the cross and died for our sins, but is that all? No! Thank God for Good Friday, but what we really celebrate at Easter is the Resurrection and the truth which Paul states in the second part of Romans 6:23—"But the free gift of God is eternal life in Christ Jesus our Lord." Every child of God is in Christ and therefore spiritually alive right now. We skip over this truth when we hear and believe only half a gospel, and so again we miss out on the richness of our identity in Christ.

As mentioned before, we also fail to know who we are in Christ because of the state of academia, where I (Neil) have labored as a student and seminary professor much of my life. For many years, I had the sense that most of the effort was spent in writing papers that nobody was reading and answering questions that nobody was asking. The battle cry seemed to be "We need scholarship!" After earning five degrees (including two doctorates), I can say that I'm committed to higher education, and I believe that each one of us also needs to "be diligent to present [ourselves] approved to God as [workmen] who [do] not need to be ashamed, handling accurately the word of truth" (2 Timothy 2:15). However, I think the battle cry should be "We need life, godliness, knowledge of the truth and a humble dependence upon our heavenly Father!" Good Christian scholarship should produce those things, which would be key to knowing who we are in Jesus and to experiencing unity with one another.

MINISTRY IN LOVE

After praying that truth and unity would characterize His followers, Jesus prays that love also would be our trademark: "I have made Thy name known to them, and will make it known; that the love wherewith Thou didst love Me may be in them, and I in them" (John 17:26). Earlier in His ministry, when Jesus was asked to identify God's greatest commandment, He said, "'You shall love the Lord your God with all your heart, and with all your soul, and with all your mind.' This is the great and foremost commandment. The second is like it, 'You shall love your neighbor as yourself.' On these two commandments depend the whole Law and the Prophets'" (Matthew 22:37-40). Christian education, however, often has the wrong goal and often has made doctrine an end in itself. When we do that, we distort the very purpose for which good doctrine was intended.

If we clearly understood and carefully obeyed the message of the Bible, our relationship with God and our relationships with our fellow human beings would be transformed. Paul declared, "The goal of our instruction is love from a pure heart and a good conscience and a sincere faith" (1 Timothy 1:5). It is discouraging to think that students can graduate from seminary purely on the basis that they answered most—not even all—the questions right. A person can do that and not even be a Christian! That kind of knowledge "makes arrogant, but love edifies" (1 Corinthians 8:1). In academia, if not the world at large, we end up extolling the virtues of the theologian and the apologist at the expense of the one who wins souls and loves the Lord and others. Scripture says, "He who wins souls is wise" (Proverbs 11:30, *NIV*), and "By this all men will know that you are My disciples, if you have love for one another" (John 13:35). Furthermore, the Bible's requirements to be a leader in the church are all based on godly character and a knowledge of God's truth.

Too much of our message is nothing more than a subtle form of Christian behaviorism which sounds something like this: "You shouldn't do that; you should do this. That isn't the best way to do it; here is a better way." So we try harder and end up huffing and puffing our way to burnout. We have only succeeded in moving from negative legalism ("Don't do this and don't do that!") to positive legalism ("Do this, do this, and do this!"). Where is the life of Christ in this? Where is His love that frees and heals, that speaks truth and unifies?

Let me illustrate. Never in the history of the Church has there been a more concerted effort to save our marriages and our families. Various programs on marriage, parenting and divorce recovery have sprung up in our churches. Parachurch ministries designed to support the family have surfaced everywhere. Christians are flocking to get their psychology degrees and counseling licenses. Books on marriage and parenting dominate the best-seller list. Why? Because saving our marriages and our families is the greatest felt need in America today. With all this concerted effort, how are we doing? Have marriages gotten healthier and families stronger? Sadly, the state of marriages and families seems to be getting worse. Why aren't these books, programs, ministries and experts accomplishing more?

To answer that question, consider that most of the practical instruction on Christian living comes from the second half of Paul's epistles. Having in the first part of his epistles established theologically that we are complete in Christ, Paul then goes on in the second part of his letters to tell us how to behave as children of God. When we don't understand and appropriate the first half of Paul's epistles, our attempts to behave as the second half instructs will fail. Pure behaviorism based on a principle or law that calls for obedience cannot produce what the life of Christ can, which we respond to by faith according to what God says is true and then to live by the power of the Holy Spirit. Paul writes, "Our adequacy is from God, who also made us adequate as servants of a new covenant, not of the letter [of the law], but of the Spirit; for the letter kills, but the Spirit gives life" (2 Corinthians 3:5,6).

Most believers aren't firmly rooted in Christ. If they were, they could be built up in Him and then walk in Him (see Colossians 2:6). Tragically, many Christians don't have any idea who they are as children of God and are struggling under bondage to any number of things. Their spiritual growth will be severely restricted until they are free in Christ. When these children of God are established free in Christ and filled with His Holy Spirit, they will do almost instinctively what the second half of Paul's epistles instruct. Such freedom in Christ and the Spirit's leading will help heal marriages and strengthen families.

Jesus said "By this is My Father glorified, that you bear much fruit" (John 15:8). Desiring to glorify our Heavenly Father, we expend considerable effort to bear fruit, but often end up fruitless. Why? Because Jesus teaches, "I am the vine, you are the branches; he who abides in Me, and I in him, he bears much fruit; for apart from Me you can do nothing" (John 15:5). The fruit you bear is evidence that you are abiding in Christ. We can't bear fruit without abiding in Christ no matter how hard we try.

This is so subtle because the instruction from the second half of Paul's epistles can be very good. Without realizing it, we shift our confidence in God to confidence in our programs, our strategies and ourselves. We search for better programs and strategies instead of searching for God. We try to shape behavior instead of renewing our minds and submitting to our loving God so that He can develop within us a Christlike character, so that we can see in our relationship with God and with others the answer to Jesus' prayer "that the love wherewith Thou didst love Me may be in them, and I in them" (John 17:26).

At the close of His ministry, Jesus prayed for truth, unity and love among His followers, and these elements are key to our vision of God's people and His churches being free in Christ. If God Almighty is the center of our lives and our churches, we can indeed stand strong in His truth, draw together in unity, and reach this world for Christ as they recognize Him by our love. If we personally are going to be an answer to this High Priestly Prayer, we are going to have to live and minister together in truth, in unity and in love. A Freedom Ministry can help your church open itself up to the Holy Spirit's working and the power which will enable you to move towards that biblical goal.

EQUIPPING OTHERS FOR MINISTRY

The key to learning to live and minister together in truth, in unity and in love is equipping people to do the work of ministry. There are simply not enough pastors and counselors to reach even a small percentage of the Christian population. So if we don't equip lay people to do the work of a Freedom Ministry (see Ephesians 4:12), the work will not get done. Based on years of experience and our unwavering confidence in God, however, we can say that if you establish the ministry outlined in this book and use the material already prepared, your church or mission group will see many people finding their freedom in Christ. Spiritually mature and adequately trained laypeople can help 95 percent of the Christian population resolve their personal and spiritual conflicts.

Besides training laypeople to minister to one another, we Christian leaders must assume our responsibility and make sure that Christ is the center of our lives and our ministries. We must understand that Christian counseling is an encounter with God, not a humanistic self-help program. Jesus alone is the "Wonderful Counselor" (Isaiah 9:6), the great Physician, the only One who can set a captive free and bring healing to a hurting humanity (see Luke 4:18). As the Lord's bond servants, we are to depend on Him for every aspect of life and encourage others to do the same. Then the Lord will work through us and our ministries.

This book—a supplement to *Helping Others Find Freedom in Christ*—will also help you equip people for ministry. Section One explains how you can establish a freedom ministry in your church or mission. Section Two is an eight-session inductive study based on *Helping Others Find Freedom in Christ*. We encourage you to work through this section before you attempt to launch a freedom ministry. The supplemental material in Section Three, "Answers to Common Questions," and Section Four, "Glossary of Terms," will be useful as you work through the material.

THE RIGHT FOUNDATION

For any ministry to succeed, the right foundation must first be laid. The critical element of that foundation and therefore of the success of a freedom ministry is the acceptance and support of your church leadership. You cannot lead a ministry of freedom in Christ without being under the authority of church leaders. Consequently, your careful and patient introduction of Freedom in Christ materials and its ministry principles is an essential first step toward building the ministry. An attitude critical of current ministry or an arrogant pushing of this material as "the only way" will invite resistance and damage possibilities for future ministry. So we encourage you to adopt a servant's heart, let God work in your life, and be willing to wait for His timing. You can't move any faster than you can educate. As some wise person has observed, "If you are one step ahead of your people, you are a leader; if you are ten steps ahead of your people, you are a martyr."

If you are a senior pastor, you have many opportunities to gently help your people recognize the importance of finding their freedom in Christ. You can, for instance, use your sermons to introduce your people to the importance of discovering the power of their identity in Christ. Like one pastor we know, you can use the 36 chapters of *Living Free in Christ* as the basis for an extended series on a believer's identity in Christ. As part of your regular training meetings, you could have your board and your staff members read and discuss some of the books or view some of the videos used in Freedom in Christ sessions. Also, have the basic books *Victory Over the Darkness* and *The Bondage Breaker* available for loan or purchase.

If you are an associate pastor, youth pastor or lay leader, you will need to work within the authority patterns and your sphere of ministry to establish the foundation for a Freedom in Christ ministry. An elder, Bible study leader or Sunday school teacher may seek permission to use the Freedom in Christ videos or *Breaking Through to Maturity*, a curriculum designed to teach adults *Victory Over the Darkness* and *The Bondage Breaker*. You might give your pastor or other church leaders a copy of *Victory Over the Darkness* or *The Bondage Breaker* and share how God has used it in your life, but don't be pushy or preachy. Also, youth editions of the essential Freedom in Christ books are available for youth pastors interested in helping young people find their freedom in Christ. As the lives of their younger brothers and sisters are changed, other church members will want to find out how to experience that freedom.

As a church pastor for nine years, I (Tom) sought and received permission to lead studies based on Neil's videos and to do weekend seminars at my church. I began walking people through the Steps to Freedom myself, and word of God's work in people's hearts and lives began to spread throughout the Church. As people's lives are changed at your church, you will have many opportunities to expand the ministry if you haven't burned any bridges by pushing too far too fast. In fact, powerful testimonies will come from laypeople whose lives have been transformed by the freedom they have found in Christ. God can work mightily when these people share with other members of the church what they have experienced.

One of the real tests of your freedom, however, will be whether you can be patient and at peace when you don't get your way or your timing. Remember that your responsibility to those in spiritual authority over you is to pray and obey (see Hebrews 13:17). Use the materials in your personal ministry and sphere of influence and trust God for the fruit. As you wait, follow Jesus' command and "let your light shine before men in such a way that they may see your good works, and glorify your Father who is in heaven" (Matthew 5:16).

Seldom will you get any positive results by suggesting that some present ministry or method isn't working. How do you get an old bone away from a dog? You don't do it by grabbing the bone. All you will end up with is a dog bite. Throw the dog a steak, and he will voluntarily spit out the old bone. That's why we have never pushed Freedom in Christ on anyone. We have never gone where we haven't been invited or spoken where we haven't been asked. Still, the ministry grows in God's way and His timing.

As the material gains acceptance among people at your church, plan to participate in a nearby conference or schedule one of your own. Freedom in Christ has several communicators available to lead a live conference or facilitate a video conference at your church. These conferences cover the material of the basic sixteen-session course and provide initial counselor training. You can also conduct your own conference using our videos and resources. Call our office at (310) 691-9128 for details and we will supply the material. At this point, you will be using a conference to both expose more people to the concept of freedom in Christ and to begin to identify those who have a special interest in the ministry and the spiritual maturity to be trained and involved.

From the start of your efforts to develop a Freedom in Christ program, be praying that God will plant the desire and vision for an ongoing freedom ministry in the hearts of church leaders and members. Every church and every legitimate Christian ministry should have at its heart the desire to see all its people living free and productive lives in Christ. Your prayers are especially significant as you plan a conference, invite key people to attend, and wait to see what seeds are planted and what fruit they bear.

After the conference is a good time to organize the ministry. Interest is very high, and often more people are interested in making personal freedom appointments than can be accommodated at the conference. If you already have trained and organized lay ministers in your church, you may choose to work within that existing organization and train them to take others through the Steps to Freedom. If your church doesn't have lay ministers or counselors, then you will need to provide enough administrative leadership to organize a new ministry. Whichever situation you find yourself in, the rest of Section One will provide the guidelines you need to establish an ongoing freedom ministry in your church.

AN OVERVIEW

The goal of a freedom ministry—helping people find and maintain their freedom in Christ—is accomplished through the development and deployment of laypeople who can lead others to freedom in Christ and disciple them. This development process involves the screening, training and oversight of leaders called "encouragers." The administration of the program also involves the screening, scheduling and shepherding of those seeking freedom. (We call them "counselees" even though no fees are charged for our services.) The diagram on page 21 illustrates the structure of the Freedom in Christ program and identifies the major areas of ministry that need to be developed. A small church may have one person who oversees the entire ministry, but a large church may need a team of several people working together.

As you undoubtedly know, competent, spiritual leadership is critical for any fruitful ministry. Gifted and talented people who are not spiritual will destroy the credibility of the ministry when their own faith falters or they fall into sin. Spiritual people who are not competent will destroy the ministry through mismanagement, misunderstanding and neglect. Unfortunately, dedicated incompetency is still incompetency. Also, every leader needs to be free in Christ before he or she can help others find that freedom. We simply cannot impart what we ourselves do not possess.

Identifying the spiritually mature *and* gifted people who can be leaders in this ministry may take some time, but this step is the most critical part of starting the ministry. (For a list of qualifications for spiritual leadership in this ministry, see pages 86-90 in *Helping Others Find Freedom in Christ*.) The Lord spent all night in prayer before He chose the Twelve, and we do well to follow His example and pray. Under no circumstances should you ask for volunteers. Instead, you must prayerfully select the people you feel God has chosen. Even when you rely on God, however, you'll quickly discover that many potential leaders have unresolved issues. Invest the time to help them mature before launching them into ministry.

Now let's look briefly at each area of ministry highlighted in the chart on page 00 and see who and what is needed to make the ministry fruitful.

ADMINISTRATION AND LEADERSHIP

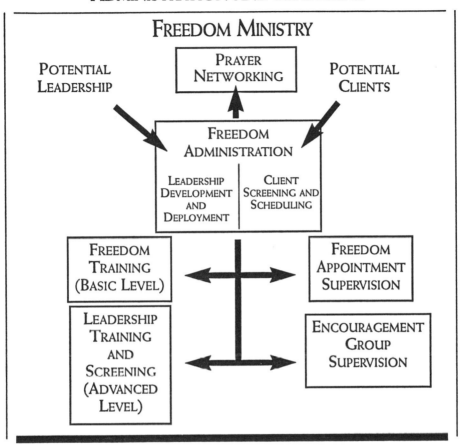

ADMINISTRATION

Our experience has taught us that someone with leadership skills and administrative ability needs to function as the overall director of a Freedom Ministry. He or she may not be the best encourager or a gifted teacher, but maturity and discernment are important personal qualities for the person in this position to possess. This person also needs to be able to get along with people, recruit others into the ministry and deal tactfully with problems that always arise in any volunteer organization. (For more information, see "Administration and Leadership," page 23.)

TRAINING

In the training program, potential lay encouragers read books, watch and discuss videos, and observe freedom appointments as prayer partners. Someone who understands the material and is experienced in leading people through the Steps to Freedom needs to lead the video discussions. However, another person may organize the training sessions and track people as they move through the process of becoming encouragers. (For more information, see "Encourager Training," page 25, and "Setting Up the Encourager Training Class," page 30.)

ENCOURAGER SCREENING

People who want to be involved in the ministry and are familiar with the material don't automatically qualify to become encouragers and have others put under their spiritual care. Allowing the wrong person into this ministry can kill it. (We've uncovered Satanists trying to infiltrate this important work!)

After much prayerful screening on your part, those people who are officially designated as encouragers must complete the first sixteen sessions of basic training and receive from those in authority the recommendation to continue. They then sit in on several freedom appointments as a prayer partner. Next, one of the trainers will watch them conduct a freedom appointment. After the potential encourager completes these assignments, the director will interview him or her and decide whether that person is ready to start meeting with others for freedom appointments. Along the way, some interested people will discover that this is not their ministry. Other people will need you to help them see that truth. Again, it's important that people going through the basic training understand that they will not automatically qualify to serve as an encourager. (For more information, see "Encourager Screening and Deployment," page 33.)

FREEDOM APPOINTMENTS

At the heart of the ministry are freedom appointments. During these meetings, an encourager leads a counselee through the guided prayer and process of repentance outlined in the Steps to Freedom. Since the average appointment lasts between three and four hours, these appointments need to be scheduled for an entire morning, afternoon, or evening. Difficult cases will take longer. (See "Freedom Appointments," page 42.)

ENCOURAGEMENT GROUPS

Following their freedom appointment, people often need the encouragement of other believers to learn to maintain their freedom and grow in the grace of God. The leaders of these groups need to be mature Christians who can disciple others. *Breaking Through to Spiritual Maturity* is the curriculum that many group leaders use to disciple counselees in their new-found freedom. In addition, we recommend that counselees read a chapter a day in *Living Free in Christ* for 36 days and then use the devotional *Daily in Christ* for one year. What counselees learn in their freedom appointments needs to be reinforced. Getting free in Christ is one thing; staying free is something else. (See "Setting Up Encouragement Groups," page 48.)

PRAYER SUPPORT AND NETWORKING

Prayer is the spiritual foundation for this ministry. Those who are committed to intercessory prayer need to intercede for everyone involved— counselees, encouragers, group leaders and administrators. A Freedom in Christ ministry can indeed be a battleground for spiritual warfare, and prayer is crucial to victory and freedom. Alongside this commitment to prayer, another priority is to make this freedom ministry available to all believers in your community by networking with pastors and inviting people outside your church to attend your training sessions. (See "Prayer Support and Networking," page 51.)

ADMINISTRATION AND LEADERSHIP

As we mentioned earlier, someone with leadership skills and administrative ability needs to direct your freedom ministry. This motivated, competent and spiritually-gifted person should coordinate the overall ministry. If an already-busy church staff member is assigned this responsibility and his or her heart is not fully in it, the ministry will fly like a turtle. Also, unless yours is a very small church, the senior pastor probably can't oversee the ministry because of other responsibilities and the fact that this task could be overwhelming. (Be forewarned! Once you have helped a few people find their freedom in Christ, you will be hooked. The difficulty will be saying no to those people you know who, by the grace of God, you could probably help.)

The director needs to oversee several major tasks:

Recruiting and training encouragers;

Scheduling freedom appointments;

Recruiting and training group leaders for follow-up discipling;

Coordinating support groups;

Ordering all necessary materials;

Reserving facilities for training, counseling, and support groups; and

Representing the ministry to the leadership of the church.

Depending on the size of the church and the ministry personnel available, a Freedom in Christ ministry can be structured in a variety of ways. In a smaller church, for instance, all the leaders will, of necessity, be volunteers. In larger churches, several of the administrative jobs listed above can and should be delegated to responsible people (perhaps a combination of staff members and volunteers) who comprise a leadership team. This team should meet every month to evaluate the ministry, formulate policy decisions, pray for one another and plan for the future. We also strongly suggest that you appoint a prayer coordinator who maintains close contact with the director. Whatever the structure of the ministry, leaders must be careful not to let demand for the ministry dictate the hours spent in the ministry. Leaders must pace themselves and those under their authority to prevent burnout.

Leaders must also work to keep the ministry before the hearts and minds of the congregation so new leaders and encouragers can constantly be recruited. One way Freedom Ministries at Crystal Evangelical Free Church of Minneapolis does this is through a color brochure which outlines the opportunities for those seeking freedom as well as for those seeking training in the ministry. We also encourage churches to schedule during their worship services, Sunday school classes or other group meetings testimonies by those finding freedom in Christ. These personal accounts not only give glory to God, but they also encourage other people to seek help.

A word of caution: Care needs to be taken that the people sharing these testimonies do not overstate what God has done. Creating false hope or implying instant maturity will damage the credibility of the ministry. The fact remains, however, that people who are struggling can be greatly encouraged when others testify that God's truth does set people free and that Jesus Christ is the way to a vital spiritual life. It's important that people sharing their stories make it clear that the Steps to Freedom do not set us free. Christ is the One who sets us free, and our response to God in repentance and faith is what sets us free.

ENCOURAGER TRAINING

The material for training encouragers includes books, study guides (which greatly increase the learning process by helping people personalize and internalize the message) and several series of video and audiotapes (each series comes with a corresponding syllabus). Obviously, trainees receive the most thorough training when they watch the videos, read the books and complete the study guides. Some trainers, however, choose not to use the videos and instead use only the books and study guides.

Overviews of Basic Training and Advanced Training are given below. The material should be presented in the order listed.

BASIC TRAINING		
Sessions 1–4	Sessions 5–8	Sessions 9–16
Conference or Video: "Resolving Personal Conflicts" Reading: *Victory Over the Darkness* and *Study Guide* Supplemental Reading: *Living Free in Christ*	Conference or Video: "Resolving Spiritual Conflicts" Reading: *The Bondage Breaker* and *Study Guide* Supplemental Reading: *Released from Bondage*	(See "Setting Up the Encourager Training Class," page 30.) Conference or Video: "Spiritual Conflicts and Counseling" and "How to Lead a Person to Freedom in Christ" Reading: *Helping Others Find Freedom in Christ* and *Helping Others Find Freedom in Christ Training Manual* and *Study Guide*

Successful completion of Basic Training also requires that trainees do the following:
- Go through the Steps to Freedom with an encourager.
- Participate in two or more freedom appointments as a prayer partner.
- Meet the leadership qualifications established by your church.
- Be recommended by the director of the freedom ministry.

Only after completing the coursework, gaining some hands-on experience under the observation of the ministry's leaders and being recommended by them as a new encourager is a trainee ready to help others find freedom in Christ.

SCHEDULES FOR BASIC TRAINING

A sixteen-session format would require sixteen two- to three-hour week-ly meetings. Showing two video lessons each night will require about 12 sessions for the first three video series. During each of the last four ses-sions, you would use one of the four hour-long videos in the "How to Lead a Person to Freedom in Christ" series. This schedule does not include much time for discussing the books, the inductive studies, or the content of the video series. Such discussion could take place at another meeting time (Sunday morning has worked for some people), or you could discuss the material after showing the video. This 16-session approach is summarized in the following chart:

Sessions 1–4	Sessions 5–8	Sessions 9–16
Resolving Personal Conflicts	Resolving Spiritual Conflicts	Spiritual Conflicts and Counseling and How to Lead a Person to Freedom in Christ
Two video lessons each night.	Two video lessons each night; the last tape presents the Steps to Freedom, which trainees can do together in class or individually with an encourager.	Two video lessons each night for four sessions; one hour per night for the final four sessions.

Another possible schedule involves showing one video series on a Friday night and Saturday each month. With this approach—which requires only one facilitator giving one weekend each month—you cover all the mater-ial in four weekends. Generally, however, there is less time to discuss the videos with this schedule, but trainees could meet Sunday morning or one night during the week to discuss the books and the inductive studies.

Weekend #1	Weekend #2	Weekend #3
Resolving Personal Conflicts	Resolving Spiritual Conflicts	Spiritual Conflicts and Counseling
Friday Night— Video lessons 1-2, Saturday— Video lessons 3-8	Friday Night—Video lessons 1-2, Saturday— Video lessons 3-7 and the Steps to Freedom	Friday Night—Video lessons 1-2, Saturday—Video lessons 3-8

On the fourth weekend, which uses the shorter video series "How to Lead a Person to Freedom in Christ," you could meet only on Saturday.

Crystal Evangelical Free Church models a third approach to training. They conduct a series of video conferences which is open to anyone and advertised through other churches in the community. Each month, they show the first half of the three video series on one Saturday and the second half of the three series on another Saturday. (In essence, they show half of three seminars simultaneously on six Saturdays spread over three months.) It takes two Saturdays to complete each video series, and all three can be completed by attending the six Saturday sessions. The church shows the three series simultaneously because many people have not completed all of them. Here is an example of a previous schedule:

Resolving Personal Conflicts The material in *Victory Over The Darkness and Study Guide*	Resolving Spiritual Conflicts The material in *The Bondage Breaker* and *Study Guide*	Spiritual Conflicts and Counseling—The material in *Helping Others Find Freedom in Christ* and *Helping Others Find Freedom in Christ Training Manual and Study Guide*
Part 1—The first four videos 8:30 a.m. to 3:30 p.m. First Saturday, Third Saturday and Fifth Saturday	Part 1—The first four videos 8:30 a.m. to 3:30 p.m. First Saturday, Third Saturday and Fifth Saturday	Part 1—The first four videos 8:30 a.m. to 5:30 p.m. First Saturday, Third Saturday and Fifth Saturday
Part 2—The second four videos 8:30 a.m. to 4:30 p.m. Second Saturday, Fourth Saturday and Sixth Saturday	Part 2—The second four videos 8:30 a.m. to 5:30 p.m. Second Saturday, Fourth Saturday and Sixth Saturday	Part 2—The second four videos 8:30 a.m. to 5:30 p.m. Second Saturday, Fourth Saturday and Sixth Saturday

Crystal Evangelical Free Church charges $15.00 for each two-part seminar for a total cost of $45.00 for all three training conferences. They charge this fee, first and foremost, to encourage the commitment to complete each series and, second, to cover the costs of the syllabus, copied materials and refreshments.

This extended format allows plenty of time for discussion, but it requires three video set-ups and three skilled seminar leaders who will commit six Saturdays to the ministry in the fall and again in the spring, factors which a smaller ministry may not be able to handle.

Once an encourager has completed Basic Training and been involved in the ministry, he or she may desire more advanced training, and Freedom in Christ has materials dealing with specific issues. These topics can be covered in an additional training course (see below), special meetings or regularly scheduled encourager meetings.

ADVANCED TRAINING
Material should be studied in the order listed.

Sessions 1–4	Sessions 5–8	Sessions 9–12	Sessions 13–16
Book: *Walking in the Light* Subjects include: Divine and counterfeit guidance, discernment, fear, anxiety, how to pray and how to walk by the Spirit	Book and Video Series: *The Seduction of Our Children* Subjects include: What our children are thinking and experiencing, discipline, parenting styles, how to pray for your children and how to lead them to freedom in Christ Supplemental reading: *To My Dear Slimeball*	Book: *A Way of Escape* Subjects include: How people get into sexual bondage and how they can become free in Christ	Can include one of the following: Book: *Overcomers in Christ* (in process) Subjects include: The nature of substance abuse and how the bondage can be broken in Christ Supplemental reading: *How You Can Establish an Overcomers in Christ Ministry in Your Church* (in process) Book and Video Series: *Setting Your Church Free* Book: *Setting Your Marriage Free* (in process) Book: *Spiritual Warfare* by Dr. Timothy Warner Video series: "Resolving Spiritual Conflicts and Cross-Cultural Ministry" also by Dr. Timothy Warner

We realize that whatever schedule you choose for Basic Training and however you handle Advanced Training, you have a lot of material to cover. (In my "Resolving Personal and Spiritual Conflicts" conferences, I [Neil] take a full week to cover almost all of the Basic Training material.) Know, however, that there are no shortcuts to establishing educated and effective lay leaders for your ministry. Again, while you may decide to open these training meetings to all who will commit the time, make it very clear that attending the seminars does not automatically qualify a person to participate in the ministry.

We must mention here, however, that around the world many people are using this material without any formal training to lead others to freedom in Christ. After all, Jesus Christ is *the* Bondage Breaker, and the process is not a matter of technique but of truth, character and humble dependence upon God. The kind of training outlined above enhances the Spirit's work; it does not replace it. Such training helps people overcome their fears and gain confidence in their ability to lead others to freedom, but there is no substitute for Spirit-dependent living.

Also, be aware that this training brings to the surface a lot of issues in people's lives. Some folks will find it very difficult to even read the books. Be prepared to lead many potential encouragers through the Steps to Freedom while their training is in process.

Furthermore, it would be naive to think there will be no spiritual opposition to this ministry. After all, Satan hates the truth and deplores the light, and, unfortunately, so do people who have something to hide. Therefore any ministry that calls people to walk in the light and speak the truth in love is going to encounter opposition. If someone feels the threat of being exposed, that person will flee the light or try to discredit the light source just as the Pharisees did in their confrontations with Jesus. The more deadly and subtle of these attacks appear to be theological: someone will take issue with a point of the law. In the vast majority of cases, the problem has its roots in petty jealousy, selfish ambition or a personal issue that has not been resolved. And in every case, don't be defensive. Instead, handle the opposition with gentleness, patience and truth.

This inevitable spiritual opposition to the work of Christ underscores the importance of having your team of encouragers meet regularly for prayer, instruction and feedback. Ongoing, on-the-job training is essential for any ministry, and Freedom in Christ is no exception. In fact, we have seen cases become more difficult as encouragers mature. About the time that you think you've heard it all, a case will come along and shatter all your preconceived ideas. This pattern definitely keeps us from becoming complacent and relying on our own cleverness instead of on God. This pattern also points out the need for encouragers to have the support of one another and other more experienced Freedom in Christ workers.

SETTING UP THE ENCOURAGER TRAINING CLASS

You must begin this ministry with the most mature and caring people available because a chain is only as strong as its weakest link. Be aware, however, that if you advertise a counselor training class, the majority of those who show up will be needy people looking for answers to their own problems. They are the people you are trying to help, but first you need trained people to help them. Know, too, that you will sabotage the ministry if you welcome as encouragers people who do not have a good reputation in the church. Credibility is critical for the success of the ministry. So, if you decide to allow anyone to participate in the training, state up front that attendance alone does not qualify a person to be an encourager for the church.

Since no ministry can be more productive than it is personal, the initial training meeting should be a time to get acquainted. Furthermore, because this material brings to the surface a lot of issues in people's lives, much personal ministry will be going on among your group of trainees. Take the time to develop trusting relationships and, because this is a front-line ministry that will be contested, take the time to pray.

When I (Neil) taught at Talbot School of Theology, I always began the semester course in pastoral counseling with the following exercise, and this exercise is a good start for an encourager training class. It is designed to help people begin to get to know as many people as possible in a meaningful way. It is a timed exercise, and many will not finish sharing before their time is up.

Divide the trainees into groups of three and designate each person as A, B, or C. The triads make up a larger circle as follows:

Person A always stays in the same seat, but after each sequence, Person B moves counterclockwise to the next group in the circle and Person C moves clockwise to the next group in the circle. One person is designated to share, and the other two must remain silent and listen. The leader times the exercise, giving each person in the group two minutes to respond to the first set of questions. After all three have responded, each has two minutes to respond to the second set of questions. Each of the following sequences should take twelve minutes.

A. First Sequence
1. Describe where you lived between the ages of 7 and 12. Did you enjoy those years? What good memories do you have of that period of your life? Can you recall any particular bad experience during that time?

2. Describe your church experience during your junior high and senior high school years. What public or private school teacher did you most easily relate to during those years?

-rotate-

B. Second Sequence
1. What room in your home was the center of human warmth for you when you were between the ages of 10 and 15? Describe your relationship with your parents. Were you sure of their love? How did they show their love to you?

2. Were their many fights in your family? How did you feel when people were fighting? Which member of your family did you get along with best and why?

-rotate-

C. Third Sequence
1. What is your favorite way to spend your spare time? What would you like to do in your spare time if you had the time and the money? What book other than the Bible has had the greatest impact on your life?

2. When did God become more than a word to you? Describe the time you felt closest to God.

-rotate-

D. Fourth Sequence
1. Describe your present family situation (parents? spouse? brothers

and sisters? children?). How have you worked professionally or vocationally? What schools have you attended?

2. What does the verse, "Bear one another's burdens and thus fulfill the law of Christ" (Galatians 6:2) mean? What is the law of Christ?

-rotate-

E. Fifth Sequence (Every member of the triad is to complete each sentence before the next person begins. This sequence is not a timed exercise.)

1. When I am in a new group, I....
2. I feel most rejected when....
3. I feel closest to God when....
4. The greatest thing I fear is....
5. I feel the most satisfied when....
6. My greatest need right now is....

Conclude this exercise by praying for one another in your triad.

As outlined above, this entire exercise should take less than two hours. Although the exercise may appear a little forced or canned, you will be amazed at what it accomplishes. I usually have the participants close their eyes afterwards and silently be aware of how they are feeling. Then I ask them to describe that feeling in one word and share that word with the group. Most people will be very positive about the experience, but some will feel a little threatened or intimidated. It has been my experience that these people have some unresolved issues in their pasts.

Having completed this exercise and perhaps at the beginning of the second meeting, members of the class can form their own groups of three. These triads will remain together for the duration of the training for the purpose of prayer and role playing.

At the initial meeting, the leaders should also hand out copies of the training schedule and make the required material available. The preceding section, "Encourager Training" (pages 25-30), outlines three approaches to the first eight sessions. After those sessions, have each trainee fill out the Confidential Personal Inventory in the appendix of *Helping Others Find Freedom in Christ*. They need to do this if they are going to go through the Steps to Freedom with a trained encourager, and they should do it anyway to gain a better understanding of their own physical and spiritual inheritance. You may also want each person to share his or her own story at some point in the training process. If sharing with the whole group is too intimidating, then people could tell their story to the other two members of their triad. After eight weeks of praying together, they should have developed enough trust to be able to do that.

The second eight sessions of Basic Training are outlined below. The material for these sessions is an inductive study of the book *Helping Others Find Freedom in Christ*, which is found in Section Two of this book.

Session	Chapters	Video Series
		"Spiritual Conflicts and Biblical Counseling" Subject:
1	Introduction	"Biblical Integration" and "Theological
2	1, 2	Basis for Counseling in Christ" "Walking by the Spirit" and "Surviving the Crisis"
3	3, 4	"The Process of Growth" and "Counseling in Christ"
4	5, 6	"Counseling the Spiritually Afflicted" and "Ritual Abuse"
		"How to Lead a Person to Freedom in Christ" Subject:
5	7, 8	Hearing the Story and Step One
6	9, 10	Steps Two and Three
7	11, 12	Steps Four, Five, and Six
8	13, 14	Step Seven and After Care

ENCOURAGER SCREENING AND DEPLOYMENT

Commitment to the training program described above constitutes a major part of the encourager screening process. Completion of the training narrows the field of potential encouragers to those very familiar with the material and willing to invest time in the ministry. Being an effective encourager requires more than being familiar with and enthusiastic about the material. Many enthusiastic people who have been set free using our material have suffered from bondage for so long that they need time to mature both spiritually and relationally. While they may have dramatic testimonies of gaining freedom in Christ, their own sense of discernment may not be well developed due to years of believing lies. Leaders of the ministry therefore need to make sure that those people recommended to serve as encouragers are trustworthy and mature in their faith.

At Crystal Evangelical Free Church, everyone interested in becoming an encourager must go through a careful screening process. The church has given us permission to share with you the following outline of the process as well as the forms used along the way. You also have their permission and ours to use or modify them for your own ministry.

Requirements for Freedom in Christ Encouragers:

1. Attend a conference by Dr. Neil Anderson or view the video equivalents: "Resolving Personal Conflicts," "Resolving Spiritual Conflicts," "Spiritual Conflicts and Counseling" and "How to Lead a Person to Freedom in Christ."

2. Read the following books by Neil Anderson: *Victory Over the Darkness, The Bondage Breaker, Released from Bondage,* and *Helping Others Find Freedom in Christ.*

3. Complete an Encourager Application which, in addition to basic information, asks about spiritual experience and counseling experience.

4. Have your pastor complete a Pastoral Recommendation form.

5. Attend a personal freedom appointment with a member of the encouragement team (required even if the applicant has worked through the Steps to Freedom on their own or in a group). Having a similar experience gives you deeper compassion for counselees as well as the confidence of knowing that you are not asking others to do something you are not willing to do.

6. Sit in on at least two freedom appointments as a prayer partner. Besides seeing two different encouragement styles, you will be able to recognize the necessity of prayer in a freedom appointment and experience its power.

7. Meet with two members of the freedom ministry leadership team in an Encourager Interview. In a warm, friendly and supportive manner, both team members will ask questions about your motivation and understanding of this ministry; one member will record your answers. Whether you are ready to serve as an encourager is determined at the close of the interview. Those applicants whom the team feels are not ready will be notified in person and given honest feedback in a loving manner. In obedience to Scripture and for the good of the applicant, the truth must be spoken in love (see Ephesians 4:15).

8. Once you've completed all the training, passed the interview and been invited to become an encourager, you are required to sign an Encourager Covenant, agreeing to serve in the ministry for six months and to attend the monthly encouragers' meetings.

Now, with certificate in hand and ready to be an official part of the ministry, the new encourager talks with the director about when he or she is available for freedom appointments. Since these appointments can take from three to six hours, encouragers must be realistic about their schedules and their availability.

The encourager is also expected to attend monthly meetings for support, accountability and advanced training. At these meetings, they will learn how to recognize when a counselee may need additional help or professional intervention. They will also address such issues as establishing healthy boundaries with counselees and setting personal limits to avoid burnout.

ENCOURAGER APPLICATION

This data is solely for the confidential use of Freedom Ministries. Information, provided voluntarily, will not be released to any agency or organization.

Date of Application _____

PERSONAL

Name_____
        (Last)   (First)   (Middle)

Address _____
   (Number) (Street)   (City)   (State) (Zip)

Telephone (____)_____ (____)_____
    Area Code Home #   Area Code   Work #

Birthdate _____ Sex: ( ) Male ( ) Female

VOCATION

Current occupation _____

Current place of employment _____

Address of employment _____
     (Street)   (City)   (State) (Zip)

FAMILY

Marital Status: ( ) Married   ( ) Never married
                    ( ) Widowed   ( ) Divorced

If married, spouse's name _____

Children's names & ages _____

_____

EDUCATION

Last grade of high school completed _____

College _____ Degree _____ Date _____
                    (Name)

Graduate School_____ Degree _____ Date _____
                    (Name)

COUNSELING EXPERIENCE

Counseling Program _____ Years of participation _____
                    (Name of Program)

Professional Practice _____ Years of practice _____
                    (Clinic Name)

Prior training through Freedom Ministries? ( ) Yes   ( ) No

Describe: _____

Why do you want to be trained by Freedom Ministries to be an encourager?

_____

_____

SPIRITUAL EXPERIENCE

Church currently attending: _____

Current ministry or areas of service (if applicable)_____

_____

How long have you been a Christian? _____ How did you become a Christian?

_____

_____

Signature _____ Date _____

Office Use Only

Evaluation Date _____ Evaluated by: _____

   ( ) Approved as an encourager   ( ) Redirected to another ministry

PASTORAL RECOMMENDATION

Dear Pastor:

The person named below has applied to become an encourager in Freedom Ministries and been trained to guide others through the Steps to Freedom in Christ. Encouragers need to be spiritually mature, free in Christ, living a balanced life, and committed to the authority of Scripture and the study of God's Word. As the next step in the application process, we would appreciate receiving from you an honest assessment of the candidate. All information will be held in confidence.

Name_____

Address_____

City_____State _____ Zip _____

Telephone ( )_____

Church Name_____

Church Telephone (   )_____ Pastor's Name_____

a) How long have you known the applicant?

b) Is the applicant now or has he/she recently been under church censorship or discipline? Explain.

c) As far as you know, has the applicant ever been involved in the occult?

d) How long has the applicant been a believer?

e) From your perspective, what is his or her level of spiritual maturity? Support your answer.

f) Does the applicant have problems submitting to leadership or the authority of others? If so, describe.

g) In conclusion, I
        (   ) Strongly Recommend
        (   ) Recommend with some reservation
        (   ) Do not recommend at this time that this applicant be accepted
        to minister in guiding others through the Steps to Freedom in Christ.

Signed _____ Position _____

Date _____

ENCOURAGER INTERVIEW

Date: _____

Candidate: _____ Marital Status: _____

Interviewer: _____ Interviewer:_____

_____ Interviewers introduce themselves and welcome the candidate.

_____ Open with prayer.

_____ Explain to the candidate that this interview does not determine whether or not he or she will participate in this ministry. The interview helps the candidate and the leadership committee discern if this is the right time for the candidate to begin this type of encouragement ministry.

1. Why do you want to become an encourager?

2. Tell us a little about your spiritual journey (i.e. salvation, significant times of growth).

3. What do you do to keep yourself spiritually healthy?

4. In what capacities are you involved in your church?
5. Neil Anderson defines strongholds as "mental habit patterns of thought burned into our minds over time or from the intensity of traumatic experiences." What have been some strongholds in your life? (Look for issues like self-esteem, absentee father, God's love.)

   To what extent are you free of them—and how have you come to this point?

6. What areas are you struggling with personally at this time? (Look for attitudes toward God, self, and others.)

7. In the past, how have you resolved anger, marital discord, bitterness, and/or resentment? Give a specific example.

8. Have you been involved in the occult?

   Have you had any experience in a cult? If so, when?

   How did you remove yourself from those situations? How have you dealt with the consequences of your involvement? (Be sure the candidate is completely free from these experiences.)

9. If divorced: Was your divorce recent? What were the issues around your divorce?

   How did you deal with these issues?

10. Have you read *Victory Over Darkness* and *The Bondage Breaker*? What did you learn from the books?

    What was your opinion of their messages?

11. What personal qualities, abilities and spiritual gifts will help you be an encourager?

12. What aspects of this ministry might be difficult for you? Explain.

13. What is your view of:
    a. Homosexuality

    b. Promiscuity

    c. Depression

    d. Abortion

    e. Sexual abuse

    f.   Satanic ritual abuse

    g. Multiple Personality Disorder

14. When did you first become aware of the reality of Satan and his forces at work in the world?

15. What experience have you had in spiritual warfare?

    How do you deal with spiritual attacks?

16. Explain what Neil Anderson means by the phrase "truth encounter" as opposed to "power encounter."

17. Are you willing to use the truth encounter model of ministry as an encourager? Why or why not?

18. Are you willing to submit to the authority of the leadership of Freedom Ministry?

19. Are you willing to commit to the encouragement ministry for six months and attend a monthly meeting for support, accountability, and additional training?

_____ Conclude the interview by thanking the person for his or her time and for openly, honestly answering the questions.

_____ After the candidate has left the room, make your recommendation below:

Based on this interview and our experience as encouragers, we recommend that _____

        be an encourager without reservation.
        be an encourager with some reservation. (Please explain.)

        not be an encourager at this time. (Please explain.)

Signed: _____ Date: _____

FREEDOM APPOINTMENTS

Freedom appointments are opportunities for Jesus Christ, *the* Bondage Breaker, to touch people with His truth and free them from whatever bondage they've experienced. During the freedom appointment, an encourager carefully guides the counselee through a process of prayer and repentance, and a prayer partner is usually present for spiritual support. These appointments should be centrally scheduled either by the director or another leader who is able to match each counselee with an appropriate encourager. This central scheduling prevents encouragers from burning out and screens out counselees who are not serious about taking personal responsibility for their freedom. (For a detailed discussion of these freedom appointments, refer to the chapter "The Freedom Appointment" in *Helping Others Find Freedom in Christ*.)

SETTING UP THE APPOINTMENT

To schedule a freedom appointment, a counselee first completes and returns a Confidential Personal Inventory in the appendix of *Helping Others Find Freedom in Christ*. Filling out the inventory makes counselees begin to take responsibility for their freedom and brings to the surface areas they need to deal with in a freedom appointment. The director then contacts the counselee to make sure he or she is reading *Victory Over the Darkness* and *The Bondage Breaker* or watching the videos. This investment of time and energy is essential preparation for the freedom appointment. In some cases, people experience interference while they are reading the books or watching the videos. In those cases, working through all the material before the appointment may not be possible. The critical factor is to know that the counselee is making an honest effort to prepare for the appointment.

While the counselee is getting ready for the freedom appointment, the director will be matching counselee and encourager according to gender, age, life experience and the severity of the problems. Men should work with men and women with women. On the rare occasion where it is not possible, the counselee should agree in advance to having someone of the opposite sex as an encourager. When that's the case, it is mandatory—for a variety of reasons (comfort, accountability, liability, etc.)—that the prayer partner be of the same gender as the counselee. Obviously, when counselees feel they are talking to people who understand and accept them, they will find it easier to be open and honest.

To help match counselee and encourager, the director uses the Confidential Personal Inventory to get an idea of the nature of the counselee's problems and find an appropriate encourager who has the necessary experience. Also, if the director senses—from either the inventory or the follow-up contact to make sure he or she has the necessary books—that the counselee may not be a believer, he should alert the encourager to first present the gospel and then evaluate the feasibility of proceeding through the Steps to Freedom.

In general, freedom appointments should be scheduled for times that do not have a hard and fast end point. Hurrying will short-circuit the process, which usually takes between three and four hours. Some difficult cases may take up to eight or nine hours, so beginning in the morning is usually preferable. Since the process can be emotionally draining for everyone involved, schedule some breaks. Also, the freedom appointment should be scheduled in a private, comfortable room with access to restroom facilities. (For liability reasons, most churches try to use church facilities.)

Once the match has been made, the director fills out a Record of Freedom Appointment card (see the following sample) and gives it, along with the Confidential Personal Inventory, to the encourager so that he or she will know the time, the location, and any other general information he or she might need to prepare for the appointment.

AT THE FREEDOM APPOINTMENT

The encourager and prayer partner should plan to arrive 15 minutes before the start of the freedom appointment to pray and to see that the room is adequate. The encourager needs to either bring the following items or make sure they are present before the appointment begins:

1. The counselee's Confidential Personal Inventory (CPI) to be returned to the counselee after the session.
2. The Record of Freedom Appointment to be completed after the session and returned to the director.
3. The Statement of Understanding to be completed before the session.
4. A copy of the Steps to Freedom in Christ for each person present.
5. A Bible, some tissues and a notepad to make lists during Steps Three and Six.
6. A Prayer Card to be completed—with the counselee's permission—at the end of the session.

7. A "Who Am I?" card to be given to the counselee at the conclusion of the appointment.
8. A schedule of possible encouragement groups for the counselee to consider joining.

You will find samples of some of these items at the end of this section on "Freedom Appointments."

BEGINNING THE APPOINTMENT

After introductions and some friendly small talk to set the counselee at ease, the encourager briefly describes what will take place during their time together. The encourager then asks the counselee to fill out the Statement of Understanding (a sample is shown later) for liability reasons. (Minors need to have a parental permission form filled out prior to going to a freedom appointment.) If a counselee refuses to sign the form, the encourager explains that the freedom appointment cannot proceed and politely suggests that the counselee seek professional help for his/her problems. After the Statement of Understanding is signed, the encourager moves on to a brief discussion of the counselee's CPI and begins to discuss the counselee's family background.

TAKING THE COUNSELEE THROUGH THE STEPS

This process is covered thoroughly in the book *Helping Others Find Freedom in Christ*, but a few reminders to encouragers are helpful here:

*   Reassure the counselee that everything he or she says and everything that happens will be completely confidential.
*   Pray through any resistance to the truth and have the counselee take responsibility to believe and affirm the truth.
*   The process is intense. Take breaks as needed.
*   Commit to finish—if at all possible—all seven steps of the process during this one appointment.
*   Stay on track. Listen carefully but do not let the freedom appointment become merely a time for emotional venting or giving advice.

CONCLUDING THE APPOINTMENT

The encourager reminds the counselee that freedom is his or her birthright as a child of God and that maturing as God's child takes time and effort. To facilitate that maturing, counselees are then encouraged to:

- Read through the passages listed on the "Who Am I?" card, passages which address our identity in Christ.
- Study *Living Free in Christ*, which explains in detail each statement about our identity in Christ that appears on the "Who Am I?" card.
- Get involved in an encouragement group or some other support group within the church where he or she can find the ongoing support needed to stay free and to grow in Christ.
- Seek professional help if he or she is dealing with persistent defense mechanisms or if deep traumas surfaced during the session.

Next, the counselee fills out a confidential Prayer Card so others can pray for his or her continued freedom. Above all, the encourager needs to remind the counselee to keep taking every thought captive and affirming the truth of his or her identity as God's child no matter how the enemy attacks.

AFTER THE APPOINTMENT

At the conclusion of the appointment, the encourager returns the CPI to the counselee to reassure him or her of the confidentiality of the meeting. The encourager completes the Record of Freedom Appointment and returns it and the counselee's Statement of Understanding to the director. The director keeps these forms on file in a secure place for liability reasons. If the counselee has filled out a Prayer Card, this is forwarded to the Prayer Coordinator who gives it to an appropriate prayer partner committed to praying regularly for people seeking freedom.

The following forms are used by Crystal Evangelical Free Church. They are included here only as examples. You should consult an attorney in your state before using or modifying any of these forms.

RECORD OF FREEDOM APPOINTMENT

Name _____

Telephone # Day _____ Evening _____

Appointment scheduled for:

     Day _____ Time _____

Location _____

Encourager _____

Issues to deal with include: _____

_____

_____

Office Use: Appointment Completed: Y/N   Completion date:_____

Encourager _____

Prayer Partner(s) _____

Encouragement Group: Yes   No

Professional Counseling Advised   Yes   No

STATEMENT OF UNDERSTANDING

I understand that the staff of Freedom in Christ Ministries, this ministry
(_____),
and those associated with them are not professional or licensed counselors, therapists, or medical or psychological practitioners.

I understand that everything I share during this encouragement experience will be kept confidential and that I alone hold the right to release
any information that comes from this time. I am also aware that
_____ is mandated by law to
intervene if he or she suspects that a child (under the age of 18 years) or
an elder (over the age of 65 years) is currently endangered by abuse or if
I am a danger to myself or others.

I understand that I am free to leave at anytime, that I am here voluntarily, and that I am under no financial obligation.

I deem the persons leading this to be encouragers in the Christian faith,
who are helping me assume my responsibilities for finding freedom in
Christ.

(Please Print)

Name _____

Address _____

City _____ State _____ Zip _____

Phone # (H) _____ (W) _____

Signed: _____ Date: _____

PARENTAL PERMISSION FORM

I, _____, the parent or guardian of _____, a minor child (under the age of 18), do hereby grant my permission for my child to be encouraged. I understand and deem the persons leading this to be encouragers in the Christian faith, who are helping my child to assume his or her responsibilities for finding freedom in Christ. I further understand and agree that my child is here voluntarily, is under no financial obligation, and is free to leave at any time. I understand that no one in this process is functioning in a professional capacity, and I completely release them from all liability.

(Please Print)

Name of Minor Child _____ Sex _____

Name of Parent or Guardian _____

Address _____
City _____ State _____ Zip _____

Phone # (H) _____ (W) _____

Signed: _____ Date: _____

FREEDOM APPOINTMENT PRAYER CARD

Dear Freedom Ministries Prayer Coordinator,

Please ask your team to confidentially pray for the following:

_____

_____

_____

_____

_____

Request submitted by: _____

Name (Optional) _____

SETTING UP ENCOURAGEMENT GROUPS

After walking through the Steps to Freedom with an encourager, many people find new freedom from distorted and deceived thinking, freedom which enables them to absorb God's truth like never before. The enemy, however, will seek to draw them back to the lies they have believed for so long. Encouragement groups are one way to make sure each person who finds freedom has the support and input needed to renew his or her mind in truth (see Romans 12:2).

An encouragement group usually meets weekly under the guidance of a leader who has completed all the encourager training, met all the requirements to be an encourager, and has the ability to facilitate a group. The goal of these groups is to provide a secure environment where maturity can develop through accountability, teaching, discussion and prayer support. _Breaking Through to Spiritual Maturity_ is usually the curriculum for these groups. Covering in detail the material included in _Victory Over the Darkness_ and _The Bondage Breaker_ and accompanied by a leader's guide and reproducible worksheets, this material is organized into 1-1/4 to 1-1/2 hour blocks and can be used in a 13- or 24-session series. At this critical time in the life of a counselee, reinforcing basic truths about freedom in Christ is much more important than covering new material.

ORGANIZING THE GROUPS

Each group of between seven and ten people should have a leader and co-leader that matches the makeup of the group (i.e., men leading men's groups, women leading women's groups). If possible, the leader and co-leader should both be experienced encouragers who are committed to discipleship. These group leaders report regularly to the freedom ministry leadership for prayer, support and advice in dealing with difficult people or problems.

Groups should meet in private, secure settings where confidentiality is assured. Rooms in the church, professional offices or homes without children work well. Participants in the group should fill out a Statement of Understanding about the nature of the group and be committed to the group. Having them sign an Encouragement Group Covenant is one way of both encouraging commitment to the group and establishing the group's ground rules. Most group members will have read *Victory Over the Darkness* and *The Bondage Breaker*, but those who haven't finished them should commit to completing them.

RUNNING THE GROUPS

One of the most critical issues in facilitating effective groups is helping the group understand and respect boundaries. Group leaders need to address the following items:

- Let the participants know your level of commitment to them (i.e., should group members expect a call from you if they are absent?) as well as your boundaries and any limits to contact outside of the group (i.e., no phone calls at home after 8 P.M. or on Thursdays).
- Trust takes time to develop. Caution members to not get too personal too fast.
- Keep group relationships in perspective. Don't expect everyone to meet your needs—and don't try to meet the needs of everyone in the group.
- If someone does not respond to your initiation of friendship, don't take it as rejection. Choose to respect their boundaries in love.

As a general rule, once a group has met for three to five sessions, newcomers should be assigned to new groups instead of being added to existing groups. This policy will enable intimacy and trust to develop in the groups. At the designated conclusion of the encouragement groups (13 or

24 weeks), participants should be encouraged to join other ongoing groups or Bible studies within the church.

If you have an existing group or support group structure within your church, you don't need to develop a new structure for Freedom Ministry counselees. Instead, you could train some existing group leaders in this material and then designate their ongoing groups as follow-up groups for your freedom ministry. Do what works best in your church.

ENCOURAGEMENT GROUP
STATEMENT OF UNDERSTANDING

I understand that those leading this group,_____
and _____ , are not professional or licensed counselors, therapists, or medical or psychological practitioners.

I deem those people leading or present in this encouragement group, including _____,
to simply be fellow Christians and encouragers who are volunteering to help me grow in the Christian faith. Within the encouragement group, they are not serving in a professional capacity as a therapist, counselor or medical/psychological practitioner, and I release them from all professional liability or responsibility for my experience in the encouragement group.

I understand that I am free to leave the group at anytime, that I am here voluntarily, and that I am under no financial obligation other than the materials fee.

(Please Print)
Name _____ Date _____

Address_____

City_____State _____ Zip _____

Telephone (Day) _____ (Evening)_____

Signed _____

Office Use Only

Encouragement Group Leader _____

Encouragement Group Leader Phone # (W) _____ (H) _____

[Note: None of the forms used in this manual have been drafted by a legal expert. They are included only as examples. You should consult an attorney in your state for advice on the wording of the forms you use in your ministry.]

PRAYER SUPPORT AND NETWORKING

We have seen vivid examples of the importance of prayer to the Freedom Ministries. That is why we encourage weekly prayer meetings to be held in advance of Neil's conferences. At these meetings, groups of people pray for the specific needs of the conference in order to establish a prayer shield around it, and others go on "prayer walks" through the facilities where the conference will be held. The commitment to pray in advance and throughout the week of the conference often determines the quality of the conference, and most churches have learned the hard way not to stop these prayer meetings after the conference.

Similarly, in your church, weekly prayer meetings of people committed to pray for the Freedom Ministry will keep the ministry centered in Christ and led by the Holy Spirit. Several churches have reported that when prayer was resumed after a dry season the ministry ran more smoothly, counselees no longer responded negatively to delays in scheduling freedom appointments and quality facilitators were more easily found. Now at these churches, ongoing prayer groups meet to pray for the ministry as a whole and for those who turn in a Freedom Appointment Prayer Card.

Alongside this commitment to prayer, another priority is to make the freedom ministry available to all believers in your community. At their second conference, for instance, the leaders at Crystal Evangelical Free Church circulated a Freedom Networking Card. Those people in attendance who wanted to be involved in the ministry or were already involved in some way in their own church returned the cards. The freedom ministry leaders then sent each person who responded a letter requesting more detailed information about their involvement. This information helped leaders find people interested in participating in the encourager training. Freedom Ministries also sent letters to the pastors of churches which had a significant number of people participate in the conference and invited them to participate in the encourager training.

So far, the results of Crystal Evangelical Free Church's networking have been encouraging. Many churches have sent people to be trained, and since the conference 95 percent of the freedom appointments have been made by people outside the church. The long-range goal is to more actively network with other churches for prayer and other ministry events. Freedom Ministries has become a gift from Crystal Evangelical Free Church and Student Venture, Twin Cities, to the Body of Christ in that community.

FREEDOM NETWORKING CARD

Church/Organization Name _____

Director's Name _____

Address_____

City_____State _____ Zip _____

Telephone (Day) _____ (Evening)_____

Do you use Steps to Freedom in your ministry?   (   ) Yes   (   ) No
Have you attended Dr. Anderson's conference "Resolving Personal and Spiritual Conflicts"?   (   ) Yes   (   ) No
Have you attended Dr. Anderson's advanced conference "Spiritual Conflicts and Counseling"?   (   ) Yes   (   ) No
Have you ever been a lead encourager in a freedom appointment?
                                                 (   ) Yes   (   ) No

FREE TO REACH YOUR COMMUNITY

Revival. It's talked about much more than experienced. And—as Christian leaders know—it is experienced only when the Church connects deeply with the life of Christ, and only then will the Church impact the world for Him (see John 15:1-8). The Bible teaches, however, that repentance and prayer precede impact and harvest, and that is where a freedom ministry can help. Freedom in Christ Ministries exists to help you, your ministry and your people find freedom from strongholds of sin and freedom to experience the life of God in a dynamic way. People who are free in Christ will be salt and light in a dark and decaying world (see Matthew 5:13-16).

Acknowledging and believing God's truth is the key to experiencing this freedom in Christ (see John 8:32). But we have an enemy that operates powerfully through deception and lies in order to keep believers and churches in bondage to sin (see John 8:44). Individual believers must repent if they are to find freedom from the power and control of sin and be able to impact their world for Christ (see 1 John 1:5–2:6). Likewise, churches must repent corporately if they are to find freedom and impact their communities for Christ (see Revelation 2,3).

As you seek to develop an ongoing ministry that will help individuals find their freedom in Christ, recognize that a freedom ministry also helps lay the foundation for community impact. The following chart illustrates this point and lists the resources available to assist you in guiding individuals and organizations to freedom through a process of prayer and repentance.

GOALS:	INDIVIDUAL FREEDOM	CORPORATE FREEDOM
Books:	*Victory Over the Darkness, The Bondage Breaker, A Way of Escape,* and others by Neil Anderson	*Setting Your Church Free* by Neil Anderson and Chuck Mylander
Key Events:	"Resolving Personal and Spiritual Conflicts Seminar" using the individual Steps to Freedom in Christ "Spiritual Conflicts and Counseling Seminar" (also available on video)	"Setting Your Church Free Leadership Conference" (also available on video) "Setting Your Church Free Leadership Retreat" using the corporate Steps to Freedom
Ongoing Ministry:	Establishing a freedom ministry where people can go through the Steps to Freedom with a trained encourager. Help those who found freedom in Christ grow in encouragement groups. Integrate Freedom in Christ materials and principles into existing ministry structures.	Leadership prays through a prayer action plan and develops a strategy to involve the congregation in corporate repentance. Leadership regularly seeks Christ's view of the ministry and responds in specific prayer.

You've now seen the need for the Freedom in Christ ministry, its biblical foundation, and the practical how-tos you need to establish a Freedom Ministry at your own church. It is our prayer that, as you follow God's guidance each step of the way, you will find great joy in establishing and being part of a ministry that helps people find true freedom in Jesus Christ.

AN INDUCTIVE STUDY OF *HELPING OTHERS FIND FREEDOM IN CHRIST*

AN EIGHT-SESSION STUDY THAT PROVIDES A
BIBLICAL FOUNDATION FOR HELPING OTHERS
FIND THEIR FREEDOM IN CHRIST

LEADER'S GUIDE

The following guidelines will help you organize and conduct a training series which will benefit any group of interested students. The optimum-sized group is 10 to 15 individuals. A smaller group may trail off in interest unless there is a high level of commitment on everyone's part. A larger group will require strong leadership skills to help everyone participate meaningfully.

1. Decide the dates you will meet. Consider holidays or other events which might affect the continuity of attendance. In most cases eight continuous sessions of 90 minutes each is a good length of time to adequately deal with the material.

2. Encourage people to register their intention to attend, both to help you in planning and to raise their determination to be there.
   Follow up with reminder phone calls.

3. Arrange for quality child care for each session.

4. Arrange seating informally, either in one semicircle or several smaller circles of no more than eight chairs per circle.

5. Prior to the first session, provide each student with a copy of the book and a typed schedule for the series. In most cases, people will put more into the series—both at home and at the sessions—if they buy the book themselves.

6. Briefly share one or two personal ways in which this book has benefited you, the leader. This sharing should not be a sales pitch for the book.

7. If you have more than 8 or 10 students in your group, assign some of the questions to be discussed in smaller groups, then invite each group to share one or two insights with the larger group.

   Alternate large-group and small-group discussion to provide variety and to allow every student a comfortable option in which to participate. Try various combinations in forming small groups.

8. In guiding the discussions, the following tips are helpful:

- If a question or comment is raised which is off the subject, either suggest that it be dealt with at another time or ask the group if they would prefer to pursue the new issue now.

- If someone talks too much, direct a few questions specifically to other people, making sure not to put a shy person on the spot. Talk privately with the "dominator," asking for his or her cooperation in helping to draw out a few of the quieter students.

- If someone does not participate verbally, assign a few questions to be discussed in pairs, trios or other small groups. Or distribute paper and pencils and ask people to write their answers to a specific question or two. Then invite several people, including the "shy" one, to read what they wrote.
- If someone asks a question and you do not know the answer, admit it and move on. If the question calls for insight from personal experience, invite students to comment. If the question requires specialized knowledge, offer to look for an answer in the library, from your pastor or from some other appropriate resource before the next session.

9. Pray regularly for the sessions and the students. As you guide people in learning from His Word, He will honor your service and bring rich benefits into the lives of the participants.

SESSION ONE

• Read the introduction to *Helping Others Find Freedom in Christ.*
If Christ really is the answer to life's challenges, why are so many believers defeated? Where is the sense of victory that the New Testament describes in passages like Romans 8:37: "In all these things we overwhelmingly conquer through Him who loved us"? We're convinced that these questions touch on one reason why believers don't share their faith more with others: We're not sure our faith is working for us, so why export it? In this personal study, we want to take an honest look at our life and our ministry. As preparation for helping others, we want God to begin to change us. We want to enter into the abundant life Christ promised so that we can help others find their freedom in Christ.

AN HONEST LOOK AT YOUR CHRISTIAN EXPERIENCE

• On a scale of 1 (completely defeated) to 10 (completely victorious), rate how victorious you are in the following areas of your life:

	The Agony of Defeat							The Thrill of Victory		
Your struggle with problem areas of sin	1	2	3	4	5	6	7	8	9	10
Your personal thought life	1	2	3	4	5	6	7	8	9	10
Your emotional health and stability	1	2	3	4	5	6	7	8	9	10
Your communication with your spouse	1	2	3	4	5	6	7	8	9	10
Your relationship with your children	1	2	3	4	5	6	7	8	9	10
Your relationship with your close friends	1	2	3	4	5	6	7	8	9	10
Your sense of significance and worth	1	2	3	4	5	6	7	8	9	10
Your sense of security and acceptance	1	2	3	4	5	6	7	8	9	10
Your walk with God and devotional life	1	2	3	4	5	6	7	8	9	10
Your character development	1	2	3	4	5	6	7	8	9	10

• Pick one of the areas you rated high and briefly explain why you have a sense of victory in that area. What are some of your strengths in that area?

• Now choose one of the areas you rated low and briefly explain why you have a sense of defeat about that area of your life. What are some of your weaknesses in this area?

• As you think about helping others, what fears about your own ability do you have? You may, for instance, fear that you won't be able to answer all the questions you are asked.

We believe that Christ can bring the sense of victory that we all seek and help us develop an unshakable belief in the adequacy of the gospel. But we must look intently to Him and His Word to find this sense of victory and this confidence in the gospel. As a step toward that end, take a look now at some of your foundational beliefs and how they affect you and your ministry.

A LOOK AT TWO CRITICAL DEFICIENCIES
Several years ago, as a seminary professor, I (Neil) started asking what's wrong with our western-world orientation to ministry and Christian living. I discovered two critical deficiencies. The first is an ignorance of who we are in Christ.

• As you reflect on your own Christian experience, describe the mental, emotional and spiritual impact the following statements about your identity in Christ have had on your life. Does your experience with God fit with your understanding of who He is based on these passages? Give an example. Has there been a change in the way you experience your relationship with God as you have grown to understand your identity in Christ? Describe.

"God has sent forth the Spirit of His Son into our hearts, crying, 'Abba! Father!'" (Galatians 4:6).

"The Spirit Himself bears witness with our spirit that we are children of God" (Romans 8:16).

"He chose us in Him before the foundation of the world, that we should be holy and blameless before Him" (Ephesians 1:4).

"There is therefore now no condemnation for those who are in Christ Jesus" (Romans 8:1).

The second deficiency in our western-world orientation to ministry and Christian living is that our view has all but excluded the reality of the spiritual world. As a result, many churches have gravitated to one of two extremes (stated below) regarding the spiritual dimension of people's problems. As you consider your own thinking and church background, mark two spots on this continuum: where you used to fit and where you think you fit now.

Problems such as addictions, disorders, panic attacks, depression and obsessive thoughts are demonic, and the cure is usually deliverance.	Problems result from a combination of spiritual, natural and psychological causes. Treatments must address all areas. treatment.	Problems such as these have natural or social explanations, and the solution is usually medical or psychological

• Read Ephesians 6:10-13. Are there some specific struggles that you have had in the past that you now believe had a spiritual dimension? How did

Satan operate in these struggles? Be specific about the ways he used temptation, deception and accusation.

• What other factors were involved in the struggles you just identified?

• How have you dealt with these problems in the past? What would you do differently if you were dealing with those problems today?

A LOOK AT FIVE FOUNDATIONAL PRINCIPLES
• Freedom in Christ Ministries and all our resources are built on five basic assumptions. Examine your commitment to these foundational principles by reading the following passages and answering the questions.

1. 2 Timothy 3:16,17 — Scripture is the only reliable guide for faith and practice. Identify some specific changes you've made in your life as a result of God's inspired Word giving you truth to live by (doctrine) or challenging you to a new direction in life (reproof, correction, training in righteousness).

2. Colossians 1:27-2:10 — All counseling and discipleship concepts and procedures must be based on the finished work of Christ. In Christ, you and I have all we need to grow to maturity. Explain how your critical needs for significance, security and acceptance have been met in Christ. Of these three needs, which represents the greatest ongoing struggle for you? Why do you think this is the area of greatest struggle?

3. John 16:7-15 — In our ministry, we rely totally on the present ministry of the Holy Spirit. If one day the Holy Spirit were removed from your life, what difference would it make in your walk with the Lord? Your marriage? Your ministry? Your church? Be specific.

4. Galatians 3:1-5—People will find help for their problems to the degree that they choose to respond to God in faith. Twice Paul uses the phrase "hearing with faith" to describe the initial and life-changing response of the Galatian believers. However, these believers are now trying to find life-changing power in what they do (works of the law) rather than in what they believe. Why is personal responsibility to choose to believe God—rather than merely trying to perform better—the only starting point for internal change?

5. Hebrews 10:17-25—All growth is best accomplished with the support of the Christian community. In what ways can the Body of Christ encourage loving and sacrificial living? How critical is the support of fellow believers to your spiritual growth? How has this kind of support impacted your growth as a believer? Give examples.

• Of these five principles, which one is the most challenging to you right now? Why?

• Complete the Confidential Personal Inventory (Appendix E) in *Helping Others Find Freedom in Christ.*

BEFORE YOU MOVE ON...
• What have you learned about God in this session? What truth about God mentioned here is most encouraging to you today?

• What have you learned about yourself in this session?

• What ideas and truths discussed in this session will help you in your ministry of helping others find freedom in Christ?

SESSION TWO

• Read chapters 1 and 2 in *Helping Others Find Freedom in Christ.*

Many issues of Christian maturity involve finding balance between extremes. One example is the place of faith and works in a believer's life. Works can never gain us acceptance with God (see Ephesians 2:1-10), but works are part of God's very plan for our lives as believers. As James says, "Faith, if it has no works, is dead" (2:17). Good works are the result of living by faith according to what God says is true.

The same need for balance comes with thinking through the issue of integrating sound biblical teaching and psychology. Two extremes must be avoided. First, elevating secular theories and research to the level of Scripture in finding solutions to help hurting people. Second, dismissing helpful research that does not compromise a biblical worldview or biblical solutions to the problems people face.

With that need for balance in mind, examine the biblical perspective on natural and special revelation and discover why we must find our fundamental answers in God's Word.

A LOOK AT A "BALANCED" PSALM

• Psalm 19 praises both the works of God—His creation (vv. 1-6)—and the Word of God (vv. 7-14), natural and special revelation, respectively. Read Psalm 19:1-6. What can you learn about God from observing the heavens and the order of the universe?

• Are there any suggestions in Psalm 19:1-6 about how people can be right with God? What does your answer imply about the limitations of natural revelation in providing solutions to our problems?

• Now read Psalm 19:7-14. List the ways in which God's Word gives us answers to human problems.

• Think of a time in your life when specific passages of Scripture provided insights and guidance through some difficult problems. Briefly describe the problem and then list the passages that were helpful.

• What does the experience you referred to in the preceding question suggest about where we should primarily seek answers and solutions to human problems?

A LOOK AT THE HUMAN CONDITION

• Read Romans 1:18-32. According to this passage, is the natural person generally moving closer to or farther away from God? What does verse 18 say about the reason human beings reject God and face His wrath? Is the reason theological, scientific or moral? Explain.

• Look carefully at verses 18-23. What is the difference between ignorance (not knowing the truth) and rebellion (rejecting the truth)? Which is being described in this passage?

• *Helping Others Find Freedom in Christ's* description of the place of natural law in our society (page 25) is based on the concept that God's created order brings with it a sense of morality (see verses 19,20). In verses 26 and 27, how does Paul apply this concept of natural law to homosexual behavior?

• Look again at verses 21, 22, 28 and 32. What do these verses imply about human reasoning as a way to find solutions to human problems? What does this teaching imply about the limitations of using secular social sciences as the basis for godly solutions to the problems of a fallen humanity?

• In what ways have you tended to rely on your own ability to reason and find solutions to your problems instead of relying on God through prayer and the study of His Word? Give some specific examples.

THE SOURCE OF TRUTH
• Read Hebrews 1:1-3 very carefully. In what two ways has God clearly spoken to us?

• Explain how Christ is the ultimate revelation of God and the primary means by which He communicates to us.

• Read John 1:1-4. John expands this idea that Jesus is God's ultimate communication to us by calling Him, "the Word," but Jesus came to give us *more* than information about God. According to verse 4, why is Jesus the *only* answer to men who are separated from God and darkened in their understanding?

LOOKING AT THE WORLD THROUGH BIBLICAL EYES
• If someone said they saw something in their room that frightened them, were hearing voices and having blasphemous thoughts, what would you see as the possible sources of the problem?

Your answer to the preceding question is determined largely by your understanding of reality and how the world operates, and this view of the world has been shaped by your educational background and the culture in which you were raised. Dr. Timothy Warner, Senior Vice President with Freedom in Christ Ministries, has identified the following three different worldviews—held by people around the world—concerning the relationship between the natural world and the spiritual world.

ANIMISM
Animism is the belief that the world is pervaded with an impersonal spiritual power which is morally neutral and can be controlled by human beings for good or evil. According to this view, personal spirits inhabit our world and impact almost every aspect of life. If a Creator God exists, He is almost completely removed from human experience. Success in life

therefore depends on controlling both the impersonal spiritual power and personal spirits through specialists called shamans, medicine men, witch doctors, channelers, mediums, witches, etc. These specialists are like electricians controlling this spiritual power through spells, incantations and other occult practices. Animism can be pictured in this way:

CREATOR GOD

1. Mana-Impersonal Spiritual Power
2. Personal Spirits
2a. Good-Evil (Spirits can be good or evil.)
2b. Nature (Such as tree spirits, mountain spirits and river spirits.)
2c. Ancestors

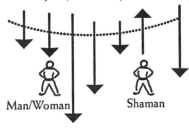

Man/Woman   Shaman

Material World

The arrows represent influence or effect. The (for the most part) unseen world can perform or effect things in the natural world. The shaman, channeler, astrologer or magician can influence the unseen world as well.

Animism is the most popular and fastest-growing worldview today. With the rise of the New Age in our culture, you can expect to encounter more and more people with this perspective. Simply changing the terms "medium" to "channeler" and "demon" to "spirit guide" does not change their function.

• Even some Christians believe that almost every sin or problem is caused by a particular demon and that the solution is to exorcise that particular demon. How is this thinking similar to animism?

• What are the dangers of this preoccupation with spirits?

• Read 1 John 4:1-6. From a biblical perspective, are there neutral spirits or neutral spiritual forces? Explain.

WESTERN WORLDVIEW
The western worldview or, since it is on the decline even in the West, the Enlightenment worldview, allows for the spiritual and natural realms. Since the two realms are so far removed from each other, the reasoning goes that our focus should be on the realm of nature and scientific study. Problems almost always have natural explanations and, with enough research, we can find the solutions. If God or spirit beings exist, they function outside the natural order and have virtually no impact on the world today. A gap between spiritual and natural exists because we no longer need spiritual explanations for anything. For the most part, these spiritual ideas are part of an old mythology used to explain the world before the Enlightenment and the rise of science. Dr. Warner pictures the western worldview this way:

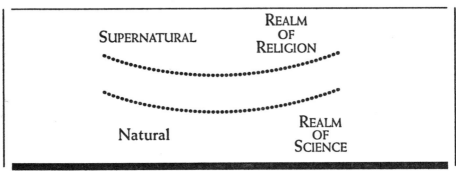

SUPERNATURAL   REALM OF RELIGION

Natural   REALM OF SCIENCE

Dr. Paul Heibert at Trinity Evangelical Divinity School refers to this perceived gap between the spiritual world and the natural world as the "excluded middle." Westerners—and even many western Christians—operate as though there is no interface between the spiritual world and the natural world. Though these Christians believe in God and the reality of the spiritual world, they are very skeptical about any suggestion of spiritual causes or solutions for their problems. Even the ministry of the Holy Spirit is often presented as an afterthought.

• How has the western worldview influenced your education? How has this viewpoint affected your Christian experience? Be specific.

WORLDVIEW TAUGHT BY JESUS AND THE BIBLE

The worldview taught by Jesus and the Bible, our only authoritative source of Truth, has three functional realms: God, angels and people or things. God has created the world with natural laws, but He is also present in the world and interacting with it both directly and through created personal spirit beings called angels. The Bible contains more than 300 references to angels, some of whom have rebelled against God under the leadership of a proud angel whom Scripture refers to as Satan or the Devil. From Genesis 3 to Revelation 22, all of human experience is presented in the context of this spiritual conflict between God and Satan. Dr. Warner pictures the biblical worldview this way:

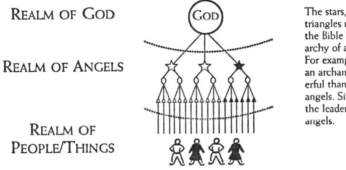

REALM OF GOD

REALM OF ANGELS

REALM OF PEOPLE/THINGS

The stars, hexagons and triangles represent what the Bible hints at—a hierarchy of angelic beings. For example, Michael is an archangel, more powerful than other lower angels. Similarly, Satan is the leader of the fallen angels.

The biblical worldview clearly acknowledges the reality of the natural world and the spiritual world operating simultaneously in tension or in harmony. The battle of all history is between the kingdom of darkness and the kingdom of light, between the Christ and the Antichrist.

• Read Ephesians 2:1-3. What sources of human problems does Paul list? Do you think Paul saw these problems as separate and distinct issues or as greatly overlapping issues? Explain what this view implies about finding solutions to human problems and why it is implied.

• What is the central solution Paul describes in Ephesians 2:4-9?

The following diagram illustrates a balanced, biblical approach to human problems which addresses their spiritual, theological, natural and psychological dimensions. We are to stay as close to the center as we can, but at the same time we are to exercise tolerance for fellow believers who may have a different emphasis in ministry.

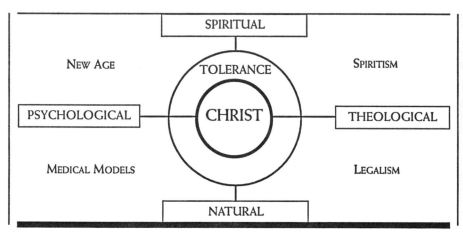

• As you reflect on your own thinking and your own ministry, which quadrant do you naturally lean toward? Why?

• Operating within the circle of tolerance, what could you gain from working with a believer whose strength and giftedness cause him or her to gravitate toward a different quadrant?

• How could the Body of Christ be strengthened if each of us learned from one another's strengths rather than attacking each other's weaknesses?

• Remember the family, described at the beginning of chapter 2, plagued with rather bizarre problems after a "biker" son returned home? The mother had a nervous breakdown, and the father began having spiritual sexual encounters. The mother, however, completely rejected the suggestion that the problems could be best understood as a spiritual conflict. Why do you think sincere, Bible-believing Christians would rather look to a secular medical or psychological model than consider a spiritual source or solution?

Some believers are afraid to consider the reality of the spiritual world, but ignoring that reality will only breed fear. More specifically, we have found in our ministry that a little knowledge about spiritual conflicts can scare people while a thorough understanding liberates them. As we explore the spiritual dimension of mental health, let's remember that the fear of the Lord expels all other fears.

Spiritual Conflict and Mental Health

According to mental health experts, you are mentally healthy if you are in touch with reality and relatively free from anxiety (page 44 of *Helping Others Find Freedom in Christ*). People under spiritual attack would probably fail on both counts. Let's explore what the Bible has to say about the battle for our minds and the problem of fear and anxiety.

Winning the Battle for Your Mind

Remember the computer metaphor? It proposes that what goes on between the ears is much like that of a computer system. The brain is the hardware while the mind is the software or program.

• The following passages describe the kind of programming built into our minds before our conversion. Who was the master programmer and what were his goals for our lives? What will our lives be like if we keep operating according to this old software?

Ephesians 2:1-3

Ephesians 4:17-19

Romans 8:5-8

• In order to grow as believers, we need to have our minds reprogrammed by the Spirit of God. According to the following verses, what critical issues need to be settled before we can effectively begin the renewal of our minds? What are the results of having our minds renewed?

Romans 12:1,2

Ephesians 4:22-24

• We need to keep reprogramming our minds according to God's Word and checking for computer viruses (evil influences). The following verses describe how believers can be affected by evil influences and what we need to do to stand against them.

How are believers affected?

2 Corinthians 2:5-11

2 Corinthians 11:3

Ephesians 4:26,27

Ephesians 6:12,16

1 Timothy 4:1

James 3:14-16; 4:6

What are believers to do?

2 Corinthians 2:8,10

2 Corinthians 10:3-5

Ephesians 4:32

Ephesians 6:10-13

1 Timothy 4:6

James 4:7,8

1 Peter 5:6-8   1 Peter 5:8,9

• As you reflect on your mental habits, what thought patterns give you
the most trouble?
Self-condemning thoughts
Fantasy
Lust
Bitter or angry thoughts towards others
Other destructive thought patterns:

• As you reflect on what you have read and studied so far, what are some
practical things you can do to begin winning the battle for your mind and
stay in touch with God's truth?

A LOOK AT FEAR AND ANXIETY

Besides being in touch with reality, mentally healthy people are relatively free of anxiety. But with Satan prowling around like a "roaring lion"
(1 Peter 5:8), we should not be surprised that fear and anxiety characterize individuals caught in spiritual conflict.

• What is the difference between fear and anxiety?

• Why is a deeper trust in God the answer to our anxieties and fears? How can that be achieved?

• The apostle John writes, "Perfect love casts out fear" (1 John 4:18). Complete the following sentences to help you identify your current anxieties or fears:

1. Lately, I have been worried about...

2. I'm afraid that...

3. One thing that concerns me is..

4. The last time I remember being afraid was..

5. I feel anxious or tense when I think about..

• Which of the following core fears has impacted your life the most? How has it hindered your growth in Christ?

The fear of rejection

The fear of failure

The fear of abandonment

The fear of death

Other fears I have struggled with:

• Work through the following "Phobia Finder" and "Anxiety Worksheet" from *Walking in the Light* (based on pages 68 and 123, respectively).

Phobia Finder

1. Analyze your fear.

   a. Identify all fear objects. What are you afraid of?

   b. When did you first experience the fear?

   c. What events preceded the first occurrences?

2. Determine where God's place in your life has been usurped.
   a. In what way do any of your fears:

   Prevent you from responsible behavior?

   Compel you toward irresponsible behavior?

   b. Confess any ways you have—either actively or passively—allowed fear to control your life.

    c. Commit yourself to God and, at the same time, accept your responsibility in dealing with your fear.

3. Work out a plan of responsible behavior.
4. Determine in advance what your response will be to any fear object.
5. Commit yourself to carrying out the plan.

ANXIETY WORKSHEET

1. State the problem you are anxious about. (A problem well stated is a problem half solved.)

2. Divide the facts from the assumptions.

    a. Identify the facts related to the situation.

    b. Identify the assumptions related to the situation.

    c. Verify the assumptions.

3. Determine what you have the right and ability to control.

a. What you can control as a matter of personal responsibility:

b. What you cannot or should not control:

4. List everything related to the situation that is your responsibility.

5. If you have fulfilled your responsibility, how can you help others?

6. The rest is God's responsibility, which—according to Philippians 4:6—we ought to commit to Him in prayer.

BIBLICAL MENTAL HEALTH

God doesn't want us stuck in fear and anxiety. Knowing who God is and who you are as His child is the key to dealing with fear and anxiety and finding true mental health. Read the following statements about God and your relationship to Him.

• How can the truths stated below—truths which a mentally healthy person knows—help resolve your specific fears and anxieties and lead to healthy mental functioning?

— God loves you (see Romans 8:35-39).

— God is able and willing to meet all of your needs (see Philippians 4:19).

— You can do all things through Christ who strengthens you (see Philippians 4:13).

— God will never leave you or forsake you (see Matthew 28:20).

— God has gone before you to prepare a place for you in heaven (see John 14:1-3).

— There is no legitimate reason to fear death (see Philippians 1:21).

— The guilt of your sins has been forgiven and there is no condemnation for you who are in Christ Jesus (see Romans 8:1).

— You are a child of God (see Romans 8:15-17).

BEFORE YOU MOVE ON...

• What have you learned about God in this session? What truth about God mentioned here is most encouraging to you today?

• What have you learned about yourself in this session?

• What ideas and truths discussed in this session will help you in your ministry of helping others find freedom in Christ?

SESSION THREE

- Read chapters 3 and 4 in *Helping Others Find Freedom in Christ*.

- The words "counseling" and "psychology" evoke almost instant reactions among believers. What are your initial thoughts and feelings when you encounter these words?

- These two words have caused unfortunate divisions in the Church. Some believers are "for" and others are "against" counseling and psychology. Consider the implications of being against counseling and psychology. The word "counsel" occurs 155 times in the King James Bible. Should believers be against seeking wise advice about living? What benefits come with seeking wise advice?

- Why do you think some Christians are opposed to counseling?

- The word "psychology" means "to study the soul." The Hebrew word for soul (*nephesh*) and the Greek word (*psyche*) occur over 700 times in the Old and New Testaments. An example is Genesis 2:7—"And the Lord God formed man of the dust of the ground, and breathed into his nostrils the breath of life; and man became a living soul" (*KJV*). Should we be against the study of what makes us truly human, the study of the source of our problems and how to help resolve these problems? What benefits come with understanding our humanness and the source of our problems?

• Why do you think some Christians are opposed to psychology?

• Read and respond to Psalm 1. What are the real issues we should be concerned about regarding counseling and psychology?

THE CHURCH'S ROLE IN MEETING NEEDS

We trust that you are committed to seeking answers to life's questions and solutions to human needs in God's Word (see 2 Timothy 3:16,17).

• As you think about people you know and about your own life, list the greatest needs we human beings have.

• What do the following passages suggest about our true needs and how we are tempted to meet these needs independently of God?

Ephesians 2:1-3

Ephesians 4:17-19

Genesis 3:1-10 (focus on verses 7 and 10)

• Read the following passages and consider the unique answer the Church has for our deepest human needs. Why does secular counseling fail to meet these needs?

John 10:9,10

Ephesians 2:4-10

• The basic human need for love most often opens the door to the Gospel and helps people connect with Christ. Why is being connected to Christ foundational to freedom and spiritual growth?

• Read the following passages. What could happen if believers and churches fail to love one another?

John 13:34,35

1 Timothy 1:5-7

1 John 3:16-19

PERSONAL RESPONSIBILITY

Loving someone does not mean that we are responsible for solving all their problems. In helping people find freedom in Christ, we are *not* trying to analyze and solve all their problems. People must assume responsibility to resolve their own problems. Instead, we are helping people connect deeply with *the* Bondage Breaker, Jesus Christ.

• What do the following passages suggest about how we should respond when people come to us for help in solving their problems? More specifically, what are their responsibilities and how can we help them fulfill those responsibilities?

Their Responsibilities   How We Can Help

James 1:5-8

James 5:13-20

HOPE FOR THE CHRISTIAN

Discipling people in Christ is exciting because, as they take responsibility for their own freedom and maturity and turn to Him, they can indeed find answers to their deepest problems. In fact, the most exciting discovery for many believers is the truth of who they are in Christ.

• All of our problems flow from either being disconnected from Christ (i.e., spiritually dead [see Ephesians 2:1-3]) or continuing to live independently of Him [see Ephesians 4:17-24]). The solution to our problems, then, is to recover life in Christ (see Ephesians 2:4-10) and to live as a new creation in Christ (see Ephesians 4:20-24). How has this truth affected your life? Be specific.

• Read Colossians 2:6-15. Note the phrases "in Him" and "with Him." What is Paul's main point about the process of spiritual growth and maturity?

Three levels of discipleship can be discerned from this passage in Colossians. We'll now look closely at each one of them.

Level I—Complete in Him: Basic Identity Issues

• Read Colossians 2:10 carefully. In what sense are you already "complete" in Christ?

• Why is understanding our identity and position in Christ the foundation for spiritual growth?

Level II—Rooted in Him: Faith Renewal Issues

• Look again at Colossians 2:7. What do the following three verb phrases suggest about our relationship to Christ and the process of spiritual growth?

"Firmly rooted...in Him"—

"Built up in Him"—

"Established in your faith"—

• Why is changing our beliefs essential if we are going to see consistent changes in our lifestyles and behaviors?

• What beliefs have you changed in the following areas that have made an impact on your life?

	Old beliefs:	New beliefs:	Changes I've experienced:
Success			
Security			
Significance			
Happiness			

Level III—Walking in Him: Changes in Lifestyle and Relationships

• Sometimes discipleship is reduced to telling someone to try harder to be a "good" Christian. What happens to believers who are trying hard to behave like Christians without changing their basic belief systems?

• What would happen to a single mother who was trying harder to discipline her children, but felt completely rejected and worthless as a mother whenever the kids were angry with her?

• Read Colossians 2:6. Walking in Christ implies living out our identity in Christ in practical ways. How would connecting with Christ as the source of her significance, security and acceptance help this single mother be more consistent in disciplining her children?

CONNECTING TO THE HUB

The following wheel diagram illustrates the point that Christian disciplines without Christ at the center will result in burnout and rebellion. Christ is the hub of the wheel. The spokes connected to the hub support the wheel and transfer the momentum to the wheel. Without the hub, the spokes would fall to the ground.

• We see most Christians operating from a law or principle basis that calls for obedience as opposed to a life basis that calls for us to respond by faith according to what God says is true—and then living by the power of the Holy Spirit. Do you agree? If so, why do you think we believers choose to live according to a law basis instead of a life-in-Christ basis?

• Read John 15:1-10. There is only one command in this entire passage about being a fruitful Christian. What is it? (See v. 4.)

• In John 15, what are we Christians compared to? What is our part in bearing fruit for Christ to the glory of God?

• What is God's responsibility as the gardener (vv. 1,2)?

• What does Christ provide as the vine (vv. 5,6)?

• Explain how prayer and obedience are aspects of abiding in Christ (vv. 7-10).

• Look at Galatians 5:22,23. Which of the fruits of the Spirit are most evident in your life?

• Which of the fruits seem to be lacking? What must you do to see God increase your fruitfulness as a believer?

• If someone is struggling and experiencing little fruit in his or her life as a believer, what is the essential thing we must do to help that person?

It's exciting to know, based on God's Word, that people connected to Christ can and will bear fruit. Furthermore, if we assume our responsibility to abide in Christ, He will use us to help others connect with Him.

• Discipleship boils down to one very simple question—"How can I be an instrument of God to help others deeply connect with the person of Christ?" Do you agree with this definition? Why or why not?

• Remember the classroom exercise in chapter 4? I (Neil) told students to write down the "most negative and damaging aspect about their lives—the last thing they would ever share with anybody or the one thing they wished nobody would find out about them." After letting them sweat a minute, I then had them identify the characteristics of the person with whom they would share such personal and painful information. What kind of person would you share your most guarded secrets with? What would that person have to be... and not be? What would he or she have to do... and not do?

• Why is it important that we become people whom others feel safe confiding in?

• What about you makes it easy for people to share with you?

• What about you makes it difficult for people to be intimate with you?

• Read 1 Corinthians 13:4-7. Which of these characteristics of love would most help others open their hearts to us?

• What basic characteristics and essential prerequisites need to be in place before we point out to someone the reality of sin in his or her life and the need for change?

• How has God shown you His love through the confrontation of a fellow believer? Be specific about the interaction, your reaction and the results of this experience.

BECOMING THE KIND OF PERSON GOD USES

Some discipleship and counseling ministries focus only on technique, curriculum, or program. We, however, believe that the primary focus should be on becoming a loving and holy instrument of God. Paul writes, "The goal of our instruction is love from a pure heart and a good conscience and a sincere faith" (1 Timothy 1:5). Then, in 2 Timothy 2:24-26, Paul describes the person God works through. Reflect on each of the following characteristics:

"The Lord's Bondservant" (v. 24)

• Why is it important that you be totally dependent upon Christ when you try to help others?

• Read Proverbs 3:5,6. What will happen if we "lean on our own understanding" as we try to help others?

• Why can trusting in Christ give us confidence about helping others?

"Must Not Be Quarrelsome" (v. 24)

• Describe how defensiveness hinders good communication.

• What happens when our goal becomes trying to win an argument?

"Kind to All" (v. 24)

• Why will hurting people shut down or withdraw if they feel criticized or rejected?

• What are some practical ways to express kindness and acceptance as you help people work through their problems?

"Able to Teach" (v. 24)

• What do we need to be able to teach when we seek to help others?

• What are some of the lies you believed that have held you in bondage? What teachings have helped you find freedom from those lies?

• Read John 8:32. Why is it so essential that we know the truth when we try to help others?

"Patient When Wronged" (v. 24)

• If someone reacts defensively to the truth being presented in the discipleship process, what are key ways you can demonstrate patience?

• Dealing patiently with people implies a commitment of time. Why do you think we are often reluctant to invest the time necessary to help people work through critical issues to a certain degree of resolution?

"With Gentleness Correcting Those Who Are in Opposition" (v. 25)

• How does Jesus describe Himself in Matthew 11:29?

• Why is gentleness essential to the ministry of helping people find freedom in Christ?

"If perhaps God may grant them repentance leading to the knowledge of the truth, and they may come to their senses and escape from the snare of the devil, having been held captive by him to do his will" (vv. 25,26).

• How does knowing that only God can bring true repentance free you from feeling responsible for the bad choices of the people you are helping?

• Why is repentance the starting point for finding freedom from "the snare of the devil?"

• Grade yourself (from "A" to "F") on the following traits of a person through whom God works:

___ Total dependence upon God
___ Not quarrelsome
___ Kind
___ Able to teach
___ Patient when wronged
___ Gentle

• Which characteristic above do you believe you need to work on the most? In what specific ways can you develop your intimacy with God to become more like Him in these areas?

A NEW APPROACH TO CHRISTIAN COUNSELING

I (Neil) am proposing an approach to Christian counseling that is identity based, resolution oriented and Spirit guided. We have already explored the foundational need to understand who we are in Christ (the identity), so let's focus briefly on the other two key concepts.

RESOLUTION ORIENTED RATHER THAN PROBLEM CENTERED

We certainly need to understand how our problems develop, and passages like Genesis 3, Ephesians 2 and the numerous biographical stories of the Old Testament give ample testimony to the power of the world, the flesh and the devil in shaping our thinking and our behavior. Knowing what caused the problem, however, does not solve it. We must break free from the paralysis of analysis and seek solutions and resolution wherever possible.

• Read Philippians 3. As you read it, write down Paul's observations about his past, his present and his future:

Paul's view of his past:

Paul's goals in the present:

Paul's attitude toward the future:

• Paul's intense personality was no doubt shaped by his upbringing, and it changed little after his conversion. He was as zealous for the Church as he had been zealous against it, but his character, motives, thinking, goals and behavior were all radically transformed. What keys to this transformation are mentioned in Philippians 3:8-10?

• What do Paul's words in Philippians 3 and his experience imply about our focus in discipleship and counseling?

SPIRIT GUIDED RATHER THAN COUNSELOR CENTERED

Most traditional approaches to counseling rely on the skill of the counselor in securing information, discerning the problems and designing the solutions, but nobody knows you, your problems and how to resolve them better than God. We therefore believe that God's insight and wisdom should be sought by the counselee at every point in the freedom process and that we should deal primarily with what God brings into the light. Read James 1:5-8 and answer the following questions:

• Where is true wisdom found? Where do people usually turn when they have problems? Though helpful at times, why will human counsel be incomplete?

• Who is primarily responsible for seeking God's wisdom, the counselor or the counselee? Explain.

• What conditions are placed on whether or not God will grant wisdom?

• Why do you think that God's granting of wisdom is contingent upon our willingness to follow Him and His guidance?

• If we are honestly seeking wisdom and are willing to deal with what God reveals, what promise does God give us in verse 5?

• We are presenting an approach to Christian counseling that is based on divine wisdom and godly character and that results in people being connected to Christ so that He, as the "Wonderful Counselor," can give them wisdom and power for resolving their problems. Do you agree with this approach? What do you like about this approach? What, if anything, concerns you about this approach? How is this approach different from "conventional" Christian counseling?

Before You Move On...

• What have you learned about God in this session? What truth about God mentioned here is most encouraging to you today?

• What have you learned about yourself in this session?

• What ideas and truths discussed in this session will help you in your ministry of helping others find freedom in Christ?

SESSION FOUR

• Read chapters 5 and 6 in *Helping Others Find Freedom in Christ.*

In chapter 4, we examined our approach to helping people caught in spiritual bondage. Though we are to be gentle, we must at the same time teach and correct ideas that are in opposition to the truth (see 2 Timothy 2:24-26). Here we will explore three essential truths that must be embraced in order to find our own freedom and to help others connect to Christ.

FIRST, FREEDOM IS FOUND IN BELIEVING THE TRUTH, NOT IN OBEYING THE LAW.

Ironically, people who appear concerned about defending the Word of God seem most opposed to any approach to spirituality or Christian maturity that moves beyond conforming observable behavior to biblical standards. The Pharisees and the scribes (spiritual lawyers) were such people. Read Luke 11:37-46.

• What is the Pharisees' approach to the spiritual life and to enforcing the spirituality of other people?

• What problems with the Pharisees' approach does Jesus point out?

• Why do you think Jesus speaks so harshly here?

• Read Luke 11:47-54. How do legalists respond to those who confront them with the truth that spirituality is found in internal change, not merely cleaning up your act?

• Why would a legalist try to avoid the light or discredit the source of the light? See John 3:16-21 and note that, in John's writing, the word "deeds" refers not just to external behavior, but to the external and internal fruit of one's relationship with God.

• Where is true freedom found?

SECOND, GOD HAS GIVEN US AUTHORITY TO HELP OTHER PEOPLE FIND FREEDOM.

In the passage we just studied, Jesus says to the lawyers, "You have taken away the key of knowledge" (Luke 11:52). Jesus is not talking about intellectual ability or the number of facts one can recall. He is talking about entering into the truth of grace through faith in Christ, truth which we must incarnate and not just memorize. When we enter into this life of Christ, we are given spiritual authority (keys) to help others also enter in.

• Read Matthew 16:16-19. What is the foundation of our spiritual authority?

• What must we believe to receive spiritual authority (see vv. 16,17)?

• Over whom do we have spiritual authority (see v. 18)?

• How broad is our authority? Does verse 19 imply limits to our spiritual authority? Identify both the scope and the limits of spiritual binding and loosing.

• In commenting on Matthew 16:16-19, Matthew 18:18-20, John 20:23, and similar passages, I (Neil) have said, "We are called by God to do His will. We are assured of God's presence for the purpose of discerning His will when two or three are gathered together in His name. Heaven—not us—initiates the binding and loosing, which we have the privilege of announcing" (page 106). I then apply this principle of binding and loosing to spiritual strongholds (i.e., the gates of hell). How have some people gone beyond the authority they have in Christ?

• According to the following passages, why do we need spiritual authority and why must we know how to exercise it over the enemy if we are to help others find freedom in Christ?

Matthew 28:18-20

2 Corinthians 4:3,4

2 Corinthians 10:3-6

THIRD, FREEDOM IS FOUND BY WINNING THE BATTLE FOR YOUR MIND.

We need to use our spiritual authority to help others win the battle for their minds, and the area which Satan works hardest to distort is our view of God. In Genesis 3, Satan succeeded in tempting Eve because he got her to doubt the goodness of God. With that in mind, read what one victim of satanic ritual abuse wrote in her diary minutes before a suicide attempt:

Dear God,

Where are You? How can You watch and not help? I

hurt so bad and You don't even care. If You cared, You'd make

it stop or You'd let me die. I love You, but You seem so far away. I can't hear You or feel You or see You, but I'm supposed to believe You're here. Lord, I feel them, see them, and hear them. They're here. People tell me You're here, but I can't tell. I'm sorry if I'm that bad, Lord, but I'm trying. Please love me and help me! I want to be a part of You. Why won't You help me do that? I know You're real, God, but they are more real to me right now. You know how real they are, Lord, but no one will believe me. Please make someone believe me, Lord. I'm alone in this, and it hurts so bad. Why, Lord? Why? I have no answers, but I have so many questions. Why won't You give me some answers? Why won't You make it stop? Please, Lord! Please! If You love me, You'll let me die.

A Lost Sheep

• List all the lies this woman has believed.

• How do you think she would describe her God?

• Put an X along the following continuums to indicate how you used to think of God. Put an O to indicate your present perception of God.

Loving and caring   Hateful and unconcerned
_____|_____|_____|_____|_____|_____|_____|_____|

Good and merciful   Mean and unforgiving
_____|_____|_____|_____|_____|_____|_____|_____|

Steadfast and reliable   Unpredictable and untrustworthy

|___|___|___|___|___|___|___|___|

Extends unconditional grace   Grants conditional approval

|___|___|___|___|___|___|___|___|

Present and available   Absent when needed

|___|___|___|___|___|___|___|___|

Giver of good gifts   Takes away, kills joy

|___|___|___|___|___|___|___|___|

Nurturing and affirming   Critical and impossible to please

|___|___|___|___|___|___|___|___|

Accepting   Rejecting

|___|___|___|___|___|___|___|___|

Just, fair and impartial   Unjust, unfair and partial

|___|___|___|___|___|___|___|___|

• How did your relationship with your parents impact your view of God? Be specific.

• How can our teaching and preaching be limited if people aren't connected to the Lord and instead hold false beliefs about Him?

• As you reflect on your Christian experience, what has helped you gain a true perception of God? Be specific.

Sometimes Satan uses mental intimidation to keep people in bondage. They may hear voices threatening them or others. Most often the power of Satan's lies is broken by simply sharing the incorrect thought with someone and affirming God's truth. Since the devil is a liar and deceiver, truth is our greatest weapon.

• As we take thoughts captive and use our spiritual weapons (see Ephesians 6:10-17), we can experience an abiding freedom in our walk with God, and that is far different from the merely external conformity produced by legalism. How has knowing this truth impacted your walk with God? Be specific.

• As encouragers, what can we do to help others maintain control of their thought lives and win the battle for their minds?

Ministry is effective when we depend on God, and nowhere is this more true than when we function as encouragers in helping others find freedom in Jesus Christ, the only true Bondage Breaker. In a freedom appointment (described in chapter 6), we want to bring someone into a vital connection with Christ through a process of prayer and repentance.

• People who desire to go through the Steps to Freedom must be prepared and committed to trust God for their freedom. Why is assuming this personal responsibility to trust God essential for their freedom?

THE NEED FOR HUMILITY AND BROKENNESS

Wait for God to prompt the people who need to go through the Steps to Freedom to approach you. When they do, have them prepare for the freedom appointment by working through the material in *Victory Over the Darkness* and *The Bondage Breaker* (video and audiotapes of these books are also available). The story of David will help you understand why we make these recommendations.

• David wrote Psalms 32 and 51 after committing adultery with Bathsheba and murdering of her husband Uriah. Why do you think God waited many months before sending the prophet Nathan to confront David? (See 2 Samuel 12:1-7.)

• Read Psalm 32:3,4. What was David experiencing when he wrote these words?

• Now read verses 5-7. How did David find freedom from this torment?

• Do you think David would have been ready or able to honestly deal with his sins had he not experienced the discipline of God for many months? Why or why not?

• What might have happened if Nathan had confronted David prematurely?

• Have you ever tried to confront someone before he or she was ready to change? What happened?

• What happens when we try to function as someone else's conscience or play the role of the Holy Spirit?

• Now read Psalm 51:1-17. Why are brokenness and humility essential to finding freedom from the bondage of sin?

• Why does trying to atone for our sin by our own sacrifice interfere with what God wants to teach us (vv. 16,17)?

DEPENDENCE ON PRAYER

Like humility and brokenness, prayer is essential to freedom appointments. We recommend that appointments involve prayer partners for two reasons. The first reason is prayer itself; the apostle Paul testifies to its importance. After discussing in Ephesians 6:10-17 the nature of the spiritual battle and our spiritual armor, Paul continues in verses 18 and 19:

> With all prayer and petition pray at all times in the Spirit,
>
> and with this in view, be on the alert with all perseverance
>
> and petition for all the saints, and pray on my behalf, that
>
> utterance may be given to me in the opening of my mouth,
>
> to make known with boldness the mystery of the gospel.

• Why is prayer essential to being strong in the Lord and resisting the evil one?

• Read Ephesians 1:17-23. As a prayer partner, what should you be praying for before, during and after the freedom appointment?

• Second, we recommend that prayer partners attend freedom appointments as a way to train others and thereby multiply this ministry. Read 2 Timothy 2:1,2. Where is the source of the true power for ministry?

• According to this passage in 2 Timothy, whom can God use in ministry?

• Why is it so important to equip faithful people to carry on the ministry?

• How will training other people expand our ability to help hurting people?

MINISTRY UNDER THE LORDSHIP OF CHRIST

The beginning of a freedom appointment can be an anxious moment for everyone involved. The person seeking help is often apprehensive and may come under attack for even attempting to find freedom. Leaders may be anxious about their ability to maintain control in the appointment, especially if this appointment is one of their first. Focusing on God, His power and His authority will enable each party to conquer their fears, and that is why we focus on God's omnipotence, omnipresence and omniscience in the preface and first prayer of the Steps to Freedom. Let's examine these three unique characteristics of God, how they impact our relationship with Him and how they can give us confidence for the spiritual battle.

OMNIPOTENT—GOD IS ALL POWERFUL

People caught in spiritual conflicts sometimes feel as though God and Satan are equal but opposite powers pulling them in two directions:

Satan   God

Me

• Why are people so easily deceived about the power of Satan?

• Why would Satan want us to believe that he and God have the same power?

• What impact would this lie that God and Satan are equal but opposite powers have on our life if we believed it?

• Read Ephesians 1:18-23; 2:4-6. What four words for power does Paul use in 1:19?

• Where is Christ in comparison to the power of other rulers and authorities (demonic forces)?

• Where are you in relationship to Christ?

• In the space below, draw a picture of Christ seated at the right hand of God, the source of power and authority. Based on your study of Ephesians 1:18-23 and 2:4-6, write your name wherever you believe you are in Christ. Then write Satan's name where he and his demons are in relation to Christ.

• What fears do you have about dealing with our spiritual enemies?

• How can a true picture of God's power and authority calm your fears?

OMNISCIENT—GOD KNOWS EVERYTHING

Since our first awareness of sin in the Garden, we human beings have sought to cover our shame and guilt by hiding (see Genesis 3:7,8). Fearing rejection, we withdraw into darkness to hide from other people as well as from God. Yet walking in the light is the only way to freedom from sin and to fellowship with God and each other (see 1 John 1:7).

• Read Psalm 139:1-7. What does God know about you and your lifestyle?

• How do you respond to the truth about God's knowledge of you? Is it comforting or scary or both? Explain.

• Read Psalm 139:23,24. When we are sure of God's love, His intimate knowledge of our lives becomes our main source of guidance in "the everlasting way." Therefore, as we walk through the Steps to Freedom, we invite God to reveal anything we need to understand in order to find freedom in Christ. Memories which have been repressed will often be revealed. What assurance do we have from this psalm that God can and will reveal anything and everything necessary for our growth?

• Why would God choose not to reveal something about our past that we may have repressed?

• Why does God sometimes bring things to light in stages, like peeling off the layers of an onion?

Omnipresent—God Is Everywhere All of the Time

Fear of abandonment is an issue for many people. They are worried that God will turn His back on them and walk off just as people in their lives have done. They are also afraid that Satan can get them to a place where God will give up on them. They may even fear that they have run so far from God that there is no way back.

• Read Psalm 139:7-16. How long has God been at work in your life?

• In what ways do you think He was working in your life even before you became a believer? Be specific.

• Look at verses 9-12. What promises do we have concerning God's presence with us even if we flee from Him or try to hide in darkness?

Before You Move On...

• What have you learned about God in this session? What truth about God mentioned here is most encouraging to you today?

• What have you learned about yourself in this session?

• What ideas and truths discussed in this session will help you in your ministry of helping others find freedom in Christ?

Session Five

• Read chapters 7 and 8 in *Helping Others Find Freedom in Christ.*

Step 1: Counterfeit versus Real

Counterfeit currency can be successfully circulated if two conditions are met. First, there must be people who will receive it without careful examination. Second, it must resemble the real thing closely enough to pass casual examination. Satan has been successfully circulating counterfeit spirituality for centuries because he deceptively appeals to human desires for knowledge, power, success and self-righteousness and because people will accept his lies without careful examination. According to Ephesians 2:1-3, we all bought into Satan's schemes in one way or another before we found life in Christ. Therefore, in this first step toward freedom, "Counterfeit versus Real," we renounce any past involvement in Satan's deceptive schemes of false spirituality.

The Need to Renounce and Repent

• According to the following passages, who are the actual powers behind false religions and the occult? Also, can God's people be affected by past or present involvement in these practices? Explain.

Deuteronomy 32:16-18

2 Chronicles 33:1-6

Psalm 106:34-39

1 Corinthians 10:17-22

1 Timothy 4:1

• Read Acts 19:11-20. Many of the believers had been involved in false religions and occult practices at the Temple of Artemis. Why do you think the demonic thrashing of the sons of Sceva had such an impact on these believers?

• If you were involved in false religions and/or the occult before you came to Christ, why do you still need to renounce these things now?

• What did the Ephesian believers do about their former involvement in cult and occult practices? Why?

• Why is renouncing the first step towards repentance?

• What do you see happening in verses 18 and 19—renouncing, repentance or both? Explain.

• **Renouncing**—The believers "kept coming, confessing and disclosing their practices" (v. 18). Read James 5:14-16, where the same word for "confessing" is used in the context of bringing healing to people through prayer. How can verbally confessing sin to another person be a healing experience?

• **Repentance**—Jesus teaches that true repentance involves action (Matthew 3:7,8), and this passage from Acts reports such action: "Those who practiced magic brought their books together and began burning them in the sight of all" (Acts 19:19). Why did these believers want to burn all their valuable books?

• Define repentance.

• What have you done to burn any bridges Satan may have used to control your life before you found freedom in Christ?

• Have you experienced a time of spiritual defeat because you did not burn a bridge? If so, explain what you learned from that experience. Have you since burned that bridge? If not, do so now.

• As you reflect on your past involvement in false religions or the occult, list below the lies you believed and the truth you now believe about the following topics.

Issue	Lies	Truth
Finding power or control		
Finding enlightenment or knowledge		
Finding spiritual success		
Finding material success		

THE NEED TO RESIST VERBALLY

When Satan tempted Him in the wilderness, Jesus resisted the devil verbally, quoting specific passages relevant to specific attacks, and then He commanded Satan to leave (see Matthew 4:1-11). James tells us believers to do the same when he writes, "Submit therefore to God. Resist the devil and he will flee from you" (James 4:7), and Jesus serves as the perfect model for us. But some people say that 2 Peter 2:10,11 and Jude 8 teach that believers should not stand verbally against Satan or his spiritual forces. These people could be reacting against some extreme forms of shouting out the devil or to the tendency to make light of the devil. Before we reach any wrong conclusion about how to resist Satan, let's look carefully at these passages.

• Read 2 Peter 2:9-22. Are these arrogant men Peter refers to believers or unbelievers? Why is that fact significant?

• Do the arrogant men have authority over Satan or are they really under his control (vv. 18,19)? Explain your answer.

• In Acts 19:14-16, what happened to the sons of Sceva when—as unbelievers—they tried to control demons?

• Read Jude 8,9. What did Michael do in his dispute with the devil? Whose authority did he call upon?

• Our authority in Christ is not an independent authority. It is a delegated authority that can be exercised only in Christ and under complete submission to Him. What do the following passages imply about our authority as we are seated with Christ in the heavenly place?

Ephesians 1:20,21; 2:6

Colossians 2:15

James 4:7

1 Peter 3:22

• Read James 4:7. Are we being self-willed when we submit to God and stand against Satan? Explain your answer.

STAYING FREE FROM IDOLS

The apostle John concludes his first letter with the admonition, "Little children, guard yourselves from idols" (1 John 5:21). You may have had little involvement with the obvious evil practices listed in the Steps to

Freedom, but we have all been guilty of looking in the wrong places for power, control, security and significance.

• Read Colossians 3:1-5. The word translated "greed" means "insatiable selfishness." Why would Paul call self-centered greed a form of idolatry?

• What are other ways people seek to meet their desires for power, control, security and significance apart from God?

• How does Satan use the kind of idolatry you just listed to keep people in bondage?

• Which of the kinds of idolatry you listed are a temptation and struggle for you?

• Read Colossians 3:5-11. What keys will guard you from submitting to these temptations and falling back into old practices?

STEP 2: TRUTH VERSUS DECEPTION

If Satan can get you to believe a lie, he can control your life in that area. Jesus calls him "the father of lies" (John 8:44). In the same chapter, Jesus says, "'If you abide in My word, then you are truly disciples of Mine; and you shall know the truth, and the truth shall make you free'" (John 8:31,32). As unbelievers, we were enslaved to Satan's lies, but as believers we can choose to believe the truth about God and our relationship with Him. Truth is the path of freedom.

THE NEED FOR BIBLICAL TRUTH

• Read John 17:15-17. How can truth protect us from the evil one?

• Why is believing God's truth the essential requirement for becoming more like Him? ("Sanctify" means "to make one holy like God.")

• Read Ephesians 4:11-15. Satan uses false teachers to confuse and deceive believers (see 1 Timothy 4:1). Why does learning biblical truth, applying it, and teaching it to others in a loving, supportive environment help us find new stability in life?

• Why is participation in the Body of Christ essential if we are to be grounded in the truth?

• Read Ephesians 6:13-17. The first piece of armor is truth and the last is the Word (*rhema*) of God. The Greek word "rhema" refers to the use of God's Word to verbally respond to Satan's attack as Jesus did in Matthew 4. Why is an accurate and expansive knowledge of God's Word essential to defeating Satan in each of his following schemes? As you think about each one, write down biblical truths which could help you in each situation.

Temptation—It's April 14 and you don't have the money to pay all your taxes, so you think about not reporting some of your cash income.

Accusation—You fall into a sin that has defeated you before, and you keep having the thought, *Now I've done it. God can never forgive me now. I might as well stop going to church and blow off this whole Christian thing.*

Deception—"You'll be so much happier if you can just get that next promotion. Go for it even though you'll be on the road four nights a week. Your family doesn't need you as much now that the kids are teenagers."

• Describe a specific time in your life when knowing a certain passage of Scripture enabled you to stand against the schemes of the devil.

• Read through the doctrinal statement in the Steps to Freedom and identify the biblical truths that you need to focus on the most right now in your quest for freedom and maturity.

THE NEED FOR HONESTY AND TRANSPARENCY

• Why do people caught in the bondage of addictions lie?

• What problems does lying about their addictions create for them and those around them?

• Why is coming out of denial the first step toward dealing with the problem that was once denied?

• Read Ephesians 4:25. Why do you think so many Christians try to hide their faults and problems?

• Why should the Body of Christ be the perfect environment for people to experience truly honest relationships?

• Read 1 John 1:6,7. Why is walking in the light essential to true fellowship with one another?

RENOUNCING SELF-DECEPTION AND SELF-DEFENSE

• The Bible clearly teaches that believers can be self-deceived. Give an illustration for each of the following verses:

1 Corinthians 3:18,19

1 Corinthians 15:33

Galatians 6:3

Galatians 6:7

James 1:22

James 4:17

1 John 1:8

We were all born into this world separated from God and therefore spiritually dead (see Ephesians 2:1). Consequently, we learned to live independently of Him. Even in the early, formative years of our lives, we learned how to defend ourselves in order to survive, cope and succeed. Now that we are in Christ, He is the only defense that we need, but those patterns of self-defense, those patterns of the flesh, are still programmed into our memories.

• Some of the more common defense mechanisms are listed below. What statement of truth from each passage listed below can set us free from these strongholds?

Denial—an attempt to protect ourselves by refusing to face unpleasant situations and circumstances of life: "Things aren't really all that bad. If I ignore problems, they'll go away" or "We don't have any problems here!" Read 1 John 1:7-9.

Fantasy—the gratification of frustrated desires by imaginary achievements or the creation of an inner fantasy world: "I feel better about myself in my daydreams or fantasy thoughts" or "I use pornography, romance novels, science fiction or movies to escape reality." Read 1 Peter 1:13.

Identification—increasing one's feelings of worth by identifying with another person or an institution of illustrious standing: "I feel more significant when I am with someone whom others admire." Read 1 Corinthians 3:3-9.

Reaction formation—preventing dangerous desires from being expressed by exaggerating opposing attitudes against them: "I frequently speak out against things like pornography, but secretly I have a real lust problem" or "I dislike things in others that remind me of my own weaknesses." Read Matthew 7:1-5.

Emotional insulation—withdrawing into passivity as protection from hurt: "When people start getting too close, I seem to clam up and avoid them. I keep myself in kind of a protective bubble that few people can get through" or "I'm afraid to love. I've been burned too many times." Read 1 John 3:16.

Isolation—failure to deal with the whole situation in order to live only the part that is good: "I enjoy going to church and feel good there, but I don't want to give up this relationship even though I know it is wrong" or "God is granting me great success at work, so I don't understand why my family is falling apart and my spiritual life is so dry." Read Psalm 1.

Regression—retreating to earlier developmental levels involving less mature responses: "When he starts talking that way, I just want to run and hide in my closet like I did when I was a little girl" or "I don't know what comes over me, but when things like that happen I just go ballistic and throw a temper tantrum."

Displacement—discharging pent-up feelings, usually of hostility, on objects less dangerous than those which aroused them: "I don't understand it, but when I have a bad day at work, I find myself yelling at the kids about every little thing" or "Why do I have thoughts about hating myself every time my spouse and I get in a big argument?" Read Hebrews 5:11-6:1.

Compensation—covering up weaknesses by emphasizing desirable traits or making up for frustration in one area by over-gratification in another: "Why is it when things are going bad at work or at home, all I can think about is fixing my golf swing?" or "The more tension there is in our marriage, the more compulsive I am about keeping the house clean." Read Romans 3:23,24.

Projection—blaming difficulties on other people or attributing one's own unethical desires to others: "There's no way I can be happy when you are creating so many problems in my life" or "I know what you're thinking. This won't work, so I'm giving up on the relationship." Read Luke 10:38-42.

Rationalization—attempting to prove that one's behavior is rational or justifiable: "What I did makes complete sense to me. Any thinking person would just look at these facts" or "That's not an excuse. It's just the truth." Read 1 Peter 2:21-23

The truth sets us free to the extent we choose to appropriate it through faith. Every child of God is responsible for choosing the truth, and making that choice—turning on the light of God's truth—is the only way to dispel the darkness.

BEFORE YOU MOVE ON...

• What have you learned about God in this session? What truth about God mentioned here is most encouraging to you today?

• What have you learned about yourself in this session?

• What ideas and truths discussed in this session will help you in your ministry of helping others find freedom in Christ?

SESSION SIX

• Read chapters 9 and 10 in *Helping Others Find Freedom in Christ.*

STEP 3: BITTERNESS VERSUS FORGIVENESS

Many people are locked in the prison of bitterness without realizing that the key to freedom hangs just outside the cell. Forgiveness is that key, able to unlock the power that our past pain can have over us. Still, many of us hold on to anger, giving the devil a place to operate in our lives (see Ephesians 4:26,27). Denial, suppression, withdrawal, revenge-seeking and angry outbursts only deepen the hold bitterness can have on us. That is why Paul says, "Let all bitterness and wrath and anger and clamor and slander be put away from you, along with all malice. And be kind to one another, tender-hearted, forgiving each other, just as God in Christ also has forgiven you" (Ephesians 4:31,32). Let's explore the freedom of forgiveness.

FORGIVENESS IS NOT RECONCILIATION

In this step, we ask people to deal with their anger, pain and bitterness as well as their misunderstanding of forgiveness. We clarify that forgiving the person who hurt you is a prerequisite for reconciliation, but reconciliation is not mandatory. In fact, in some situations, reconciliation is impossible or unadvisable. (What if the perpetrator has died or is part of a satanic cult?) In other situations, people need to forgive the offender and take a stand against the sin and further abuse. We have never seen a person still hanging on to hatred, bitterness, wrath, malice and slander make any spiritual progress. Extending forgiveness is an important step for such growth.

• Read Romans 12:17-21. What is our responsibility to our enemies?

• Reconciliation requires the effort of two parties. What does verse 18 imply about the pursuit of reconciliation?

• Can your freedom be dependent upon somebody you have no right or ability to control? Explain the role forgiveness plays in finding freedom.

• Read Romans 13:1,2 and 8-10. What is our responsibility to people involved in illegal abuse? Why is reporting abuse the loving thing to do in most situations?

• Read Luke 17:3,4. This passage has been used to suggest that we should not forgive unless we first see the offender's repentance. However, the context of these verses is the pursuit of reconciliation in a relationship. Christ's main point is simple: Confront sin, but stand ready to freely forgive. What happens if you confront sin while you are seething with bitterness and hatred towards the offender?

• Before we can confront the sin of another person, we need to work through our own bitterness and anger by forgiving that person from our heart. What do the following verses say about forgiveness and reconciliation?

Matthew 5:21,22

Matthew 7:1-5

Galatians 6:1

Forgiveness from the Heart

• Read Matthew 18:21-35. Jesus' point is clear: Forgive as you have been forgiven. Read verses 34 and 35. What happens to people who don't forgive from the heart?

• Read Matthew 6:12,14,15. Who suffers when we don't forgive from the heart? How is this suffering experienced?

• We can avoid forgiving from the heart in a variety of ways, some of which are listed below. Why do you think believers avoid forgiving from the heart? Which methods of avoidance have you used in the past?
— Refusing to admit being hurt
— Avoiding the pain
— Making excuses for those who caused the pain
— Waiting until you feel like forgiving

Dealing with Self and God

As we've helped people work through their anger and bitterness, we've often seen them overlook two critical names of those needing forgiveness—"myself" and "God." Hurting people often point the gun of anger at themselves or at God when trying to assign blame for their problems. When this happens, forgiveness becomes an issue—but let us clarify the terminology. You can't actually forgive God because He hasn't done anything wrong, but you can repent of your unrealistic and false expectations of Him. Likewise, you don't have the authority to forgive yourself for your own sins, but you can accept and affirm God's forgiveness for the sins you have confessed. As we help people process this step, we don't get hung up on terminology as long as the person's heart is right, as long as he or she is repenting of a wrong attitude toward God or him- or herself.

• Job is the classic example of a person being angry with God over the injustices of life. Look at the following passages. How did Job's attitude change after he was confronted by God Himself?

Before—Job 23:1-5   After—Job 42:1-6

• Job was honest in his relationship with God. Why do you think so many other believers want to deny that they are angry at God?

• How does this denial of their anger hurt their relationships with God?

• Why can admitting our anger and repenting of our false expectations and demands begin a healing process in our walks with God?

LETTING OURSELVES OFF THE HOOK

Many people are laboring under a heavy burden of self-condemnation. Even though they have confessed their sins and God has forgiven them, they mentally beat themselves up and try vainly to atone for their sins. Some believers also think they will continue to sin unless they constantly remind themselves of their failures. This preoccupation only leads to greater defeat as they wrongly reaffirm their fallen identities as sinners and conclude that they are unworthy to go before God. This self-flagellation is evidence that the "accuser of the brethren" is at work.

• Read Hebrews 10:11-18. Is our forgiveness and cleansing based on what we do or on what Christ has done? Explain.

• What is God's view of your sins now that you are in Christ? See verse 17.

• Read Hebrews 10:19-22. As people who are forgiven, what attitudes should now characterize us as we approach God?

• When Christ "died to sin, once for all" (Romans 6:10), what did He do for sins not yet committed? At the time of His death, how many of your sins were future sins?

WHOM DO I NEED TO FORGIVE NOW?

Every time we take individuals or groups through the Steps to Freedom, we personally repeat this step of forgiveness, and God frequently brings to mind someone we need to forgive. Take some time now to ask God whom you need to forgive from the heart. When you have made your list, take time to specifically forgive—from the heart—what each person did and how that action made you feel. Don't rationalize the sin or minimize the pain they caused you.

Working through the issue of forgiveness like this is not an optional exercise for believers. In fact, it should be a regular part of our prayer life. After all, Jesus gave us the following pattern for prayer in Matthew 6:9-15:

"'Our Father who art in heaven,

Hallowed be Thy name.

Thy kingdom come.

Thy will be done,

On earth as it is in heaven.

Give us this day our daily bread.

And forgive us our debts, as we also have forgiven our debtors.

And do not lead us into temptation, but deliver us from evil.

[For Thine is the kingdom, and the power, and the glory, forever.

Amen.]

"'For if you forgive men for their transgressions, your heaven-

ly Father will also forgive you. But if you do not forgive men,

then your Father will not forgive your transgressions.'"

• Encouraging people to forgive those who have hurt them is the most important step toward helping them find freedom in Christ. But you will not be able to help them unless you can give a comprehensive and biblical answer to two questions they may ask. Answer those questions now:

— What does it mean to forgive another person?

— How can I forgive that person from my heart?

STEP 4: REBELLION VERSUS SUBMISSION

While describing God's plan for our salvation, one of our staff members asked a man, "Who would you say is in control of your life right now?" "I am," the man replied, "and I like it that way."

The illusion that we are the "captains of our souls and masters of our fates" is one of Satan's greatest deceptions. When we try to control our lives, however, we are rebelling against God-given authority. We are rebelling against God and are playing right into the devil's hand. After all, Satan's ultimate lie was—and still is—"You will be like God" (Genesis 3:5). The truth is that we are all under God's established authority, and we are to live that way.

REBELLION IS A SERIOUS PROBLEM

• Read 1 Samuel 15:20-23. King Saul was a rebellious man, and when he failed to completely destroy everything as God had commanded, he rationalized his disobedience. What was God's response to Saul's rationalization?

• To what sins does Samuel compare rebellion in verse 23?

• Discuss how God's punishment fit Saul's crime.

• Can rebelliousness result in a person becoming demonically influenced? (See 1 Samuel 16:14 and 28:3-25.) Explain.

• Rebellion is failure to trust God. Once on my way to lead a group through the Steps to Freedom, for example, I (Tom) exceeded the speed limit because I had forgotten about the meeting. I was afraid of being rejected for being late, so I controlled the only thing I could to avoid this rejection—the gas pedal. How could trusting God instead of myself have changed the way I handled the situation?

• What tendency to rebel do you deal with in the following areas?

God (see Daniel 9:5,9)

Civil government (see Romans 13:1-7)

Spouse (see Ephesians 5:21-33)

Parents (see Ephesians 6:1-3)

Employer (see Colossians 3:22-25)

Church leaders (see Hebrews 13:17)

IDENTITY DETERMINES SIGNIFICANCE

The reason some people choose to rebel or fail to submit may come from a false view of their significance. If your significance as a person depends on position, title, role, authority, power or control, you may be tempted to rebel against anything or anyone who gets in the way. Nowhere is this kind of rebellion more evident than in the home.

• If a man's significance is based on his position as head of the home and maintaining authority, power and control in his family, how is he likely to respond to conflicts and disagreements with his wife and children?

• If a woman finds her significance and identity in her role as a mother, how is she likely to respond to conflicts and disagreements with her children?

• If a woman seeks to find her significance through gaining authority, power and control, how is she likely to respond to conflicts and disagreements with her husband?

• Read Ephesians 1:3-14. What phrases does Paul use to describe the true source of our significance, acceptance and security?

• Now look at Ephesians 5:21-33. Why does having our core identity issues (significance, acceptance and security) settled in Christ enable us to freely pursue our roles and responsibilities within marriage?

• Read 1 Peter 2:4-10. What phrases does Peter use to describe our new identities and the source of our significance and our value to God?

• Now look at 1 Peter 3:1-9. If our value and significance do not depend on controlling others or having authority, why will we be more free to submit, serve, understand, and bless those with whom we are in relationship?

• Read verses 8 and 9 again. Why does finding your identity and security in Christ free you from being drawn into arguments or becoming defensive?

Look again at these words from *Helping Others Find Freedom in Christ*: "Submission, authority, and control concern not only man/wife issues, or parent/child issues, or employer/employee issues. Submission is primarily a relational matter between the creature and the Creator. When we know who we are as children of God, we don't have to rebel, we don't have to dominate or control. We yield to the Lordship of Christ, secure in our position in Him, and relate to others with love and forgiveness" (p. 198). When we are free in Christ, we are free to be servant-leaders or servant-followers without needing to control or rebel.

• Scripture does teach, however, that there are times when we must obey God rather than human authorities (Acts 4:19;5:29). When a person in authority over you issues a command that would cause you to violate the will of God or prevent you from fulfilling it, then you must obey God. What should...

A child do if a parent is abusive and demands submission to immoral commands?

An employee do if the boss asks him or her to lie?

A wife do if her husband asks her to do something sexual which violates her conscience?

• What keeps you from yielding to the Lordship of Christ? What can and will you do about those roadblocks?

BEFORE YOU MOVE ON...
• What have you learned about God in this session? What truth about God mentioned here is most encouraging to you today?

• What have you learned about yourself in this session?

• What ideas and truths discussed in this session will help you in your ministry of helping others find freedom in Christ?

• Read chapters 11 and 12 in *Helping Others Find Freedom in Christ*

STEP 5: PRIDE VERSUS HUMILITY

"Pride" is indeed the ugly five-letter word with "I" in the middle, and in the spiritual dictionary, it always comes before "fall." Clearly, the object in which we place our confidence is a critical spiritual issue. Pride is putting confidence in ourselves, our abilities, and our schemes in our quest for security and significance. On the other hand, humility is confidence properly placed: it is confidence in the Lord. Let's look at how we can shift our confidence in ourselves to confidence in Christ.

PRIDE AND SPIRITUAL CONFLICT

• The Septuagint version of Proverbs 3:34 reads, "God is opposed to the proud but gives grace to the humble." What do the following passages have to say about pride?

James 4:6,7

1 Peter 5:5-9

• Read Isaiah 14:13-15, a passage which many scholars believe to be a description of Satan's fall. How many times is the word "I" used?

• What seems to be Satan's goal here?

• Read Genesis 3:1-6. What is Satan's goal for the woman? What words of temptation lead her to fall?

• As you reflect on your life, note where Satan has succeeded in getting you to place confidence in your own abilities or schemes to meet your needs for...

Honor and significance:

Happiness and security:

Love and acceptance:

• What have been the results of your efforts to meet these needs on your own? Be specific.

GOD IS OPPOSED TO THE PROUD

If Satan's goal is to get us to live independently of God, the key to defeating him is expressing our total dependence upon and confidence in God. After all, true humility is confidence properly placed in God, where it belongs.

• Look at the following list from Steps to Freedom. Rank yourself on a scale of 1 ("No problem here!") to 7 ("I consistently struggle here") to see where pride might be a problem in your life.

I have a stronger desire to do my will than God's will.
1   2   3   4   5   6   7

I'm more dependent on my strengths and resources than God's.
1   2   3   4   5   6   7

I believe that my ideas and opinions are better than other people's.
1   2   3   4   5   6   7

I'm more concerned about controlling others than developing self-control.
1   2   3   4   5   6   7

Sometimes I consider myself more important than others.
1   2   3   4   5   6   7

I have a tendency to think that I have no needs.
1   2   3   4   5   6   7

I find it difficult to admit when I am wrong.
1   2   3   4   5   6   7

I have a tendency to be more of a people-pleaser than a God-pleaser.
1   2   3   4   5   6   7

I'm overly concerned about getting the credit that I deserve.
1   2   3   4   5   6   7

I'm driven to obtain the recognition that comes from degrees, titles and positions.
1   2   3   4   5   6   7

I often think I am more humble than other people.
1   2   3   4   5   6   7

Optional: Because pride can be such a blind spot for us, you might have a trusted friend go over this list with you and get from him or her some additional insight on where you may struggle with pride.

• What actions reveal your tendency to put your confidence in yourself instead of God in the areas (listed above) you struggle with most? Be specific.

• When James writes that God is opposed to the proud (4:6), he uses a strong Greek military term. While we may often think of God removing His blessing when we sin, here He is pictured as standing against the proud with sword drawn. Why do you think God views pride as such a serious problem?

• Have you ever sensed that God was opposed to you? If so, when?

• During those times when you sensed God's opposition, could you have been trusting more in yourself than in Him? Describe the circumstances of your life and the state of your heart at those times.

GOD GIVES GRACE TO THE HUMBLE

Spiritual humility is placing your confidence in God. It is adopting the attitude of servant, not master. And God offers His divine assistance—in this context, His grace—only to those who have a servant's heart, those who have renounced self-sufficiency and turned to Him as Lord.

• Often it is only when we come to the end of our resources that we begin to discover God's resources. Have you ever come to that point in your life? If so, describe the circumstances, your spiritual struggle and the lessons you learned.

• What would you say to a self-assured person who comes to you for counsel, but won't admit to his or her pride?

Submitting to God and Resisting the Devil
• James 4:7 calls us to both submit to God and resist the devil if we want him to flee. What would happen if you tried to resist the devil in your own strength and your own authority? See Acts 19:13-16 for an example.

• Have you ever been caught in the sin-confess-sin-confess-sin-confess-"I-give-up!" cycle? What were the circumstances? And why didn't this approach work? What was missing?

• Why is confession by itself not enough?

• What beyond confession does genuine repentance entail?

• As you reflect on your own life, describe where actively resisting Satan's attempts to get you to live independently of God has made the most significant difference. Be specific.

• Despite the lessons you just referred to, in what areas of your life do you still tend to be self-sufficient? Why?

Pride is subtle and tricky. If we will constantly choose to humble ourselves before God, He will give us the insight we need to see where we are proud and the grace we need to choose to live in dependence on Him. The result will be the freedom to live without that unholy trinity of "me, myself and I" at the center of life.

STEP 6: BONDAGE VERSUS FREEDOM

I (Tom) grew up in Texas and often went to Padre Island to swim in the Gulf of Mexico. I always came back sunburned and happy. Unfortunately, some of the people who ignore the signs warning of dangerous riptides and undertows don't come back at all. Some do it just for the thrill and others are drunk. Some are strong enough to make it back in, but others aren't. The lifeguards—responsible for rescuing drowning people who ignore the signs—don't stand on the beach and holler, "You idiot! Can't you read the signs? You got yourself in this mess. Now get yourself out!" Instead, the lifeguards jump in, swim out and save the struggling swimmers when they can.

Unfortunately, some Christians look out at those believers caught in the undertow of sin and offer the condemning chorus, "You idiot! Can't you read the Bible? You got yourself in this mess! Now get yourself out!" But God has called us to a ministry of reconciliation, not condemnation (see 2 Corinthians 5:18).

A Ministry of Restoration and Reconciliation

• Read Galatians 6:1,2. According to these verses, what should our response be to those caught in the undertow of sin?

Our actions:

Our attitudes:

Our words:

Our commitment:

Our own walk with God:

Now read Galatians 6:2-5. At first glance, verse 5 may seem to contradict verse 2. The word for "burden" in verse 2 indicates an excessive weight that is too much for any person to bear alone. We are called to help these people who are too weak, people who need support and encouragement.

In contrast to this burden, the word for "load" in verse 5 is used for a soldier's pack. It is a normal load: it is an individual's personal responsibility. As we help others find their freedom in Christ, we can assist them in the struggle, but they must take responsibility for their own freedom through confessing and renouncing sin, affirming God's truth, believing in Jesus as their Savior and Lord, and taking every thought captive to Him.

• Read 2 Corinthians 5:17-21. According to this passage, who are we in Christ?

• Based on these verses from 2 Corinthians, write a brief job description for an ambassador of Christ.

Title:

Main Responsibilities:

Reports to:

Necessary Qualifications for the Job:

Helpful Qualities for Success on the Job:

UNDERSTANDING HABITUAL SIN

Many of us developed independent ways of coping with life long before we were aware of God's presence in our lives or knew about His ways. Unfortunately, many of us never move beyond the flesh in our search for significance, security, acceptance, love and happiness in life. When that's the case, we bring strongholds of sin into the Christian life.

• Look at Ephesians 4:17-19. Is it possible for believers to "walk as the Gentiles walk"? Explain.

• What solution to our sinful ways does Paul outline in verses 20-24?

• Why is embracing our new identity in Christ critical to breaking free from habitual sin?

• Look at the deeds of the flesh listed in Galatians 5:19-21. What items on that list, if any, can you identify as a pattern in your life before you knew Christ?

• Did the deed(s) of the flesh you just identified meet any lasting needs in your life? If so, which ones? If not, why not?

UNDERSTANDING SEXUAL BONDAGE
• Read 1 Corinthians 6:15-20. Here Paul uses a quote from the marriage of Adam and Eve ("and they shall become one flesh"—Genesis 2:24) to describe what happens when a man has sex with a harlot. According to this passage, what are the spiritual implications of such immorality?

• To whom does your body belong? What are the ramifications of that fact?

• In what ways can we glorify God in our bodies?

• In what ways can we glorify sin in our bodies?

• What would it be like to join yourself to a harlot and become one flesh and at the same time be one in spirit with the Lord? Discuss the possibility and the conflict.

• Read Romans 6:12-16. According to this passage, what happens to someone who continues to present his or her body as an instrument of unrighteousness? Who ends up as master?

• Can you commit a sexual sin and not use your body as an instrument of unrighteousness? Why or why not?

• Why do you think sexual bondage is so difficult for many to break?

• What kind of lies about their sexuality has Satan bound people with as a result of their ungodly sexual activity?

• Sexual bondages have to be broken and the mind renewed. Explain these two truths in relationship to the teaching of Romans 12:1,2.

• Read James 5:13-16. Here James focuses on what to do about a weakness or sickness to which there may be a spiritual dimension. A critical part of the healing process is the prayerful support of others and the sufferer's personal confession of sin (v. 16). This word for "confession" is also used in Acts 19:18 for the public confessing of occult practices (see

Matthew 3:6 and Mark 1:5 as well). Why do you think verbally expressing one's sins to another believer may be critical in breaking the spiritual
strongholds of sexual bondage?

DESTRUCTIVE BEHAVIORS

• Read John 10:1-14. Compare and contrast Jesus as the Door and the
Good Shepherd with the thief (v. 10). What did Jesus come to do? And
what does the thief want to do?

• How does the characterization of Satan as a thief in John 10 match
John's reference to him as a murderer and a liar in John 8:44?

• Based on what you know about Satan, give one or two reasons why each
of the following problems may have a spiritual component. Notice what
lies are involved, how Satan is seeking to kill or destroy, and what good
things he is trying to steal.

Homosexuality

Abortion

Suicide

Eating disorders

Substance abuse

Jesus said, "I came that they might have life, and might have it abundantly" (John 10:10). Satan's goal is to rob us of this abundant life in Christ through lies and deceit. He uses habitual sin to convince us that we can't live without the substitutes he provides. The truth is that life is found only in Christ. It's an abundant life, full of joy and freedom, but it is only enjoyed when we renounce the shameful things done in darkness and walk in the light (see Ephesians 5:3-14).

BEFORE YOU MOVE ON...
• What have you learned about God in this session? What truth about God mentioned here is most encouraging to you today?

• What have you learned about yourself in this session?

• What ideas and truths discussed in this session will help you in your ministry of helping others find freedom in Christ?

SESSION EIGHT

• Read chapters 13 and 14 in *Helping Others Find Freedom in Christ*.

STEP SEVEN: ACQUIESCENCE VERSUS RENUNCIATION

Few people deny the reality that some sins and problems seem to affect families from generation to generation. The major debate is over how these sins and tendencies are transferred between generations. Is the transfer genetic, environmental or spiritual? We believe that all three may play a role in a person's predisposition to certain sinful behaviors and addictions. However, this predisposition excuses no one for not being all that God wants him or her to be. Each of us must assume his or her own responsibility in finding freedom from the past.

OUR SPIRITUAL VULNERABILITY

Some Christian leaders respond negatively to the teaching that we can inherit spiritual problems from our ancestors. I (Neil) respond by saying that we are not guilty for our parents' sin, but because they sinned, we are vulnerable to their areas of weakness. Look at the following passages and explore how spiritual problems may be passed on from generation to generation.

• Read Exodus 20:4-6. What sin is described here?

• What do the following passages show about the connection between idolatry and demonic activity?

Deuteronomy 32:16,17

Psalm 106:37,38

1 Corinthians 10:20

• If your parents were involved in pagan idolatry, temple prostitution, demonic worship, and human sacrifice, what impact would this activity have on you and your family?

• What is the impact of people's involvement in present-day, demonically-inspired cults and occult practices on their children?

• What about God's character gives us hope for people whose families have been involved in demonic worship and the occult?

• What must the people who have been involved in these satanic activities do to return to God? What must their children do?

"To acquiesce" means to agree without consent or to passively give in. For the children to experience God's lovingkindness, they must turn from their parents' ways and choose to love Him and keep His commandments. God doesn't promise that they won't still suffer consequences for their parents' rebellion if they repent, but He does promise that they will experience His loyal love.

• How have your parents' sins affected you? What consequences have you had to deal with?

• Read Jeremiah 32:16-18. Where is the iniquity of the fathers placed?

• What does this passage imply about the transmission of problems from one generation to the next? Could the transmission be environmental? Genetic? Spiritual? Which do you think is most likely? Explain your answer.

• If the transmission of sin were strictly genetic, what hope of escape would future generations have?

• Read Leviticus 26:38-40. Whose sin must be confessed to find freedom? Why?

• What does this passage from Leviticus imply about finding freedom from the bondage handed down to us from our families?

• What could happen if we cover up our parents' sin or boast that it can't have any effect upon us?

THE SPIRITUAL DIMENSION

Ephesus was the center of many pagan religious cults and the site of the Temple of Artemis. Demonic activity was well known and part of the people's worldview. Many of the Ephesian cults and religious groups passed their writings and rituals down from generation to generation.

• Read Ephesians 2:1-3. What does this passage say about the following contributors to our sin?

Environmental factors

Direct spiritual factors

Internal factors

• Paul teaches that demonic forces are directly involved in our lives as unbelievers. If someone was once involved in demonic activity, would it be possible for that person's children to be impacted? Why or why not?

• Look once again at Acts 19:16-19. Apparently, some who had already believed under Paul's ministry (he had been in Ephesus a year or so at this point) felt it necessary to publicly renounce their former practices and burn the valuable magic books, which must have been passed down from generation to generation. Why do you think they felt this action was necessary even though they had previously believed and received forgiveness for their sins?

THAT'S NOT FAIR

As we try to help people discern where their problems may have originated, many times the problems can be traced back to childhood experiences. Some have said that it doesn't seem fair that Satan would take advantage of a child innocently playing with a Ouija board or offer a child a demonic spirit as an imaginary friend. Of course it isn't fair!

• How is Satan described in 1 Peter 5:8,9?

• What do predators do? Who in the herd do they go after? And whose responsibility is it to protect the young?

• Apply this image from nature to our responsibility as human parents. Should we expect Satan to be fair? What can we do to protect our children and teach them how to resist him?

Personal responsibility is the key to the Steps to Freedom and finding freedom in Christ. As Peter says in 1 Peter 1:13; 5:8, we must gird our minds for action and be sober, mentally and spiritually alert. We can't expect to be passive and win the spiritual battle. We must also choose to burn all spiritual bridges that the enemy could use to gain or regain access to our lives. And we must take our stand against the enemy in the power and authority of Jesus Christ, clothing ourselves in Him as our protection (see Romans 13:14).

IN CLOSING
We conclude the Steps to Freedom by reading through the list of statements which summarize a believer's new identity in Christ. The most important key to maintaining our freedom in Christ is to be firmly rooted in our identity in Christ (see Colossians 2:6,7).

IDENTIFYING THE LIES THAT FLOW FROM OUR PAINFUL PASTS
Many of the lies we have believed flow from our past relationships with significant people. In *Helping Others Find Freedom in Christ*, we therefore recommend developing a two-part "Before Freedom Identity" and "In Christ Identity" chart (p. 246 and appendix C). As part of the Freedom Appointment, I (Tom) have developed the following list as an additional way to help others identify the lies they need to renounce and the truth of their new identities in Christ.

• Go through the list below and check the lies that you believed, lies which Satan has used to shape and control your life, your view of yourself, and your view of God.

I RENOUNCE THE LIE THAT...	I ANNOUNCE THE TRUTH THAT IN CHRIST...
I'LL NEVER BE ACCEPTED BY GOD OR OTHERS.	**I'M ALREADY ACCEPTED.**
Everyone including God accepts me if I work hard to please them. All love must be earned.	God accepts me because I am His child (John 1:12).
I must be accepted by certain others to feel O.K. about myself.	I am accepted by Christ as His friend (John 15:15).
I must do everything well or right to be accepted.	I am justified, made right with God through Christ (Romans 5:1).
Sooner or later God will reject me and turn away from me.	I am united with God, one spirit with Him (1 Corinthians 6:17).
I have no real value to God, so He will reject me sooner or later. I feel worthless as a person.	He bought me with the price of His Son. I am of infinite value to Him (1 Corinthians 6:20).
I can't break free from sin because I'm just a sinner.	I'm a saint, a holy one who may struggle with sin, but need not be mastered by it (Ephesians 1:1).
No sane person would choose to love me.	God chose to love me from all eternity and to adopt me into His family (Ephesians 1:5).
God loves other Christians more than me. If I were like them, I could get closer to God.	I have the same direct access to my heavenly Father as all other believers (Ephesians 2:18).
Some things I've done can't be forgiven. God can't keep on forgiving me. I'm a hopeless case.	I have been redeemed and forgiven of all my sins (Colossians 1:14).
I have to be perfect to be accepted.	I am already complete in Christ (Colossians 2:10).

I'LL ALWAYS BE ABANDONED.	I'M ALREADY SECURE.

I'm unworthy of love and deserve to be condemned and abandoned. God is basically angry with me and always wants to punish me.

I am free forever from condemnation (Romans 8:1,2).

Sooner or later, my life always falls apart. If God really loved me, life would be easier.

I am assured that all things work together to make me more like Christ, and that is good (Romans 8:28-30).

Others tell me I'm bad or worthless, so I must be bad or worthless.

I am free from any condemning charges against me (Romans 8:31ff).

Sooner or later, God will give up on me and abandon me.

I cannot be separated from God's love (Romans 8:35ff).

My relationship with God depends on me trying harder to please Him.

I have been established, anointed, and sealed by God (2 Corinthians 1:21,22).

Sooner or later, people will find out about me and reject me, abandon me or hurt me.

My life is hidden in Christ and therefore secure (Colossians 3:3).

Since I still struggle with sin, God will quit working in my life and give up on me.

I am confident that the good work that God has begun in me will be perfected (Philippians 1:6).

I'll never know if I'm going to make it to heaven.

I am already a citizen of heaven (Philippians 3:20).

I'm afraid I'll be abandoned, so I have to be weak, meet everyone's demands or pretend I'm dumb.

I have not been given a spirit of fear but of power, love and a sound mind (2 Timothy 1:7).

When the chips are down, everyone always leaves me.

I can find grace and mercy in my time of need (Hebrews 4:16).

I can't really defeat Satan because he has me under his control.

I am born of God, and the evil one cannot touch me (1 John 5:18).

MY SIGNIFICANCE OR SUCCESS IS BASED ON SOMETHING I DO.

I'M ALREADY SIGNIFICANT.

I have nothing of real value to offer others.

I am the salt and light of the earth (Matthew 5:13,14).

The only way I can make an impact in this life is by being in control and asserting myself. My significance comes from what I do, not who I am.

I am a branch of the true vine, a channel of His life (John 15:1-5).

My life will never really amount to anything.

I have been chosen and appointed to bear fruit (John 15:16).

I have no right or ability to tell others about Christ because my life isn't perfect.

I am a Spirit-empowered witness of Christ (Acts 1:8).

Significance is found only in a beautiful appearance, superior intelligence or an image of success.

I am God's temple, significant because I have God indwelling me (1 Corinthians 3:16).

I have to be perfect for God to really use me.

I am a minister of reconciliation for God because I am His new creation (2 Corinthians 5:17ff).

If people really knew me, they would not want to work with me.

I am God's co-worker (1 Corinthians 3:9).

God has no use for me. I must put myself down or put others down to make me feel better.

I am seated with Christ in the heavenly realm (Ephesians 2:6).

I am an accident, a cosmic mistake, and therefore worthless. I wish I were someone else.

I am God's workmanship (Ephesians 2:10).

I can only be significant through much effort and hard work. I can never be really sure of God's love.

I can approach God anytime with freedom and confidence (Ephesians 3:12).

I can't change. It's just too hard, so I give up. I can't take risks because I might fail.

I can do all things through Christ who strengthens me (Philippians 3:6).

OTHER LIES I HAVE BELIEVED: OTHER TRUTHS I NEED TO
                                     BELIEVE:

• Now go back through the list. As you do so, renounce the specific lies you checked and affirm the corresponding truth of your new identity in Christ.

• Pick one or two key lies that you have believed about yourself. What new freedom are you experiencing in these areas as a result of affirming your identity in Christ?

• Where are you still struggling? Look at the biblical passages that confirm your new identity in these areas. Now write out one or two key truths about your new identity that you can use to renew your mind.

STAYING FREE IN CHRIST...

As you've seen in this study, healing and maturity take time and effort. The first step toward freedom, for instance, is choosing to forgive from the heart. We must also renew our minds so that we can, among other things, view our past from the standpoint of who we are in Christ. The book *Living Free in Christ* takes an entire chapter to explore each of the 36 statements about our new identity in Christ (listed in the right-hand column of the chart above). If, after completing this exercise, you are still struggling with lies laid down in your past, take time to study carefully the list of biblical truths. After all, only God's truth can set you free. As you end this study, know that God will richly bless the time and effort you invest in believing His truth and that, in His perfect time, you will experience freedom.

Before You Move On...

• What have you learned about God in this session? What truth about God mentioned here is most encouraging to you today?

• What have you learned about yourself in this session?

• What ideas and truths discussed in this session will help you in your ministry of helping others find freedom in Christ?

ANSWERS TO COMMON QUESTIONS

SATAN: HIS DEMONS, HIS POWER, HIS ACTIVITIES

How can I tell if what I am experiencing is demonic oppression or the flesh? How can I know whether my problem is spiritual or psychological? These questions propose a false dichotomy. Our problems are never *not* psychological. There is no time when our minds, wills and emotions are not involved or pertinent to a personal problem we're having. If we understand "psychological" to mean pertaining to the soul (Greek = *psyche*) of man, then all problems impact our humanness. At the same time, our problems are also never *not* spiritual. At no time is God irrelevant. At no time is it safe to take off the armor of God. After all, the Bible presents the possibility of being tempted, accused or deceived by our spiritual enemies as continuous.

In reality, all of our problems flow from a combination of three sources: external (the world), internal (the flesh) and spiritual (the devil). Paul presents these three not as separate problems requiring different solutions, but as greatly overlapping issues that need one major solution: the life of Christ imparted through faith (see Ephesians 2:1-10). If we believers understood this truth, we would stop polarizing into psychotherapeutic ministries that ignore spiritual realities and deliverance ministries that ignore developmental issues and human responsibility. We must take into account all of reality and strive for a balanced ministry. We must help people establish Christ at the center of their lives and understand that their identities in Christ enables them to begin the process of renewing the mind and finding freedom in Him.

Getting back to the original question, we believe there is much to be gained by exploring the spiritual dimension of whatever problems you may be facing. The Steps to Freedom are a tool to help you take responsibility for your freedom by submitting to God and resisting the devil in every major area of your life. The Steps are not, however, a substitute for ongoing discipleship and prayerful support in the process of renewing your mind.

Doesn't your ministry focus too much on demons and not enough on the flesh and the world?

We understand how it may appear so, but we believe we are moving the Church toward a more biblical worldview which openly acknowledges and addresses spiritual realities. One of the major problems that has led to the ineffectiveness of the Church today is the adoption of a western worldview which ignores, on a functional level, much of what the Scriptures teach about spiritual realities. Categorizing our problems under the labels "The World," "The Flesh," and "The Devil" is a little deceiving because it tends to give the impression that they operate independently from each other. According to Genesis 1-6, if it weren't for Satan, the world and the flesh wouldn't be problems for us.

Some believers point to James 1:14 as teaching that all sin is really the result of the flesh. But this interpretation ignores the rest of the Book of James, especially James 3:13-4:10, which clearly implies that all human conflict and worldliness has a demonic dimension (3:15) requiring us to resist the devil as part of the solution (4:7). Paul says our struggle is "not with flesh and blood" but against an organized, evil, spiritual empire that controls the world (see Ephesians 6:12) and which impacts every person born (see Ephesians 2:1-3). Satan is called the god of this world, and all the world is under his evil influence. To be sure, excessive preoccupation with the demonic can be a problem with some groups. The solution is found in living according to a completely biblical worldview with Scripture as our guide.

As we've stated over and over, recognizing a spiritual dimension to our problems does not imply a "devil made me do it" theology. Nobody emphasizes personal responsibility for finding freedom more than we do. Every New Testament passage on spiritual struggles emphasizes our personal responsibility to resist and stand firm (Ephesians 6:10-12; James 4:7; 1 Peter 5:8,9). But we must take seriously the spiritual dimension of our struggles if we are to win in the battle against the flesh and the world.

The focus of our ministry is Christ, not the devil. We instruct people *not* to call up, name or deal directly with the demonic in counseling sessions. We don't want demons to manifest; we want to manifest the presence of God. Wanting to do all things decently and in order, we teach pastors, missionaries, counselors and laypeople to maintain control and work only with the counselee.

Can believers be demon "possessed"?

The simple answer to the question as asked is "no." But the relationship of believers to the demonic is not that simple.

In the original language, "demon possession" is only one word. Some have suggested that it would have been better to have transliterated it as "demonized." If we did, then a demonized person could be defined as "one who is under the influence of one or more demons." All the passages where this word is used are in the Gospels. The word never occurs after the Cross. Consequently, we will forever lack theological precision in determining if the word "demonization" can be applied to a New Testament believer. To say the concept couldn't apply because the word doesn't occur is, at best, an argument from silence and not a definitive answer.

The answer also hinges on how you define "possessed." We have a tendency to think that if we possess something, we own it (as in "possession is nine-tenths of the law"). With that understanding of the word, the question becomes "Can a Christian be owned by the evil one?" The answer: Absolutely not! Every Christian has been bought by the blood of the Lamb (1 Peter 1:18,19). We belong to the Lord Jesus Christ, and He will never leave us. Paul writes, "You were sealed in Him with the Holy Spirit of promise, who is given as a pledge of our inheritance" (Ephesians 1:13,14).

Despite what some of our critics charge, I (Neil) have never taught that believers can be "demon possesed." The first cornerstone of our message is that believers are eternally secure in their identity as children of God. We teach that no believer is in such deep bondage that they cannot exercise their responsibility to "submit therefore to God. Resist the devil" (James 4:7). Our approach is to encourage beleivers to exercise *their* authority and responsibility as children of God to repent of sin, win the battle for their minds, present their bodies to God and resist the devil.

Even though Christ has secured our victory over our spiritual enemies (see Colossians 2:15), please don't conclude that Christians can't have spiritual problems. Some believers seem to think they are immune to spiritual attack, but the Bible clearly teaches that Satan's primary attack has always been on God's people, hoping to thwart God's plan. The Bible clearly teaches that temptation, accusation and deception are constant possiblities for believers. (The following passages describe the possible impact of evil forces on believers: Genesis 3; 1 Samuel 16:14; 1 Chronicles 21:1; Job; Zechariah 3; Matthew 16:23; Acts 5:3; 1 Corinthians 5:5; 7:5; 2 Corinthians 11:1ff; 12:7; Ephesians 4:27; 6:10ff; 1 Thessalonians 2:18; 1 Timothy 1:20; 3:6; 4:1; 5:15; 2 Timothy 2:26; James 3:15; 4:4; 1 Peter 5:7,8; Revelation 2:10; 12:17.)

A true Biblical worldview presents all of creation locked in spiritual conflict that extends from Genesis to Revelation. As believers, we are aligned with God against the "god of this world" (2 Corinthians 4:4). We have been transferred from the "domain of darkness" to the "kingdom of His beloved Son" (Colossians 1:13). In this battle for the heavenly places, the Church is God's method for extending His kindgdom and as such is Satan's prime target (see Ephesians 1:3,20; 2:6; 3:10; 6:12). The entire book of Ephesians teaches that as believers we already have everything we need to experience spiritual resources through faith and obedience in the power of the Holy Spirit. Spiritual defeat is still a real possiblity for believers who still live like unbelievers (see Ephesians 4:17-32).

We are clearly told that "our struggle is not against flesh and blood, but against the rulers, against the powers, against the world forces of this darkness, against the spiritual forces of wickedness in the heavenly places" (Ephesians 6:12). Therefore, Paul teaches it is *our responsibility* to put on the armor of God, to stand firm and to resist the powers of evil (see Ephesians 6:10-18). Peter calls the devil "your adversary" and warns believers of his intension to devour them (see 1 Peter 5:7,8). The word used for "devour" is a strong term that means "to drink down, swallow down, to eat up, or to devour."[1] For example the Egyptians were "swallowed up" by the Red Sea (see Hebrews 11:29). (See also 1 Corinthians where "death is swallowed up in victory.") Twice Paul turns believers over to Satan as severe discipline for disobedience (see 1 Cornithians 5:5; 1 Timothy 1:20). We are told to submit to God and resist the devil and that he will flee from us (see James 4:7). What happens to believers if they don't obey God's Word and choose to resist the devil? All these passages imply dire consequences for believers who ignore Satan, pretend he doesn't exist or fail to stand firm in their faith. If Satan can get you to believe a lie, he can control your life. We have been clearly warned: "The Spirit explicitly says that in later times some will fall away from the faith, paying attention to deceitful spirits and doctrines of demons" (1 Timothy 4:1).

By focusing the discussion of Satan's influence on believers on the issue of the location of the demons—whether they are internal or external—some have needlessly polarized the Church. Conservative Christians have disagreed for years about what demons can do to believers and whether this control can extend to what we normally think of as internal functions such as thinking, feeling and motor activities. We could quote authors, cite references and debate the passages, but we don't believe you could use our discipleship-counseling model regardless of your view on the location issue. Let us explain.

First, the issue of internal versus external is hard to apply in the spiritual realm. As believers, is our "skin," the armor of God, repelling demons and their activities? Or is the battle for our minds fought in a spiritual realm where spatial concepts are not the key issues? The indwelling of the Holy Spirit is primarily a "relational issue" and not a "spatial" issue because of the doctrine of the omniprescence of God. The indwelling of the Holy Spirit does not automatically keep sin and evil out of our mortal bodies (study Romans 6-8). The Corinthian believers were warned about receiving other spirits besides the Holy Spirit (see 2 Corinthians 11:3,4) even though Paul calls them temples of the Holy Spirit (see 1 Corinthians 6:19). As the temple of God was violated in the Old Testament, Paul teaches that sin can reign in the mortal bodies of those who use their bodies as instruments of unrighteousness (see Romans 6:12-16). That is why he urges us to present our bodies to God as a living sacrifice (see Romans 12:1) as the necessary prerequisite to the renewing of our minds (see Romans 12:2). The whole question of "internal versus external influence" is difficult because we just don't know exactly how the material world of the brain, body and nervous system interfaces with the spiritual realm of the mind, flesh and spirit.

Second, virtually all who carefully study this issue agree that believers can be greatly impacted by evil spirits. Authors who advocate an external-influence-only view conclude this: "The Bible itself does not give us a full description of everything demons are capable of. Because of this lack of accurate information, plus the satanic ability to deceive, plus our own shortcomings in the area of discernment, it is likely that certain activities such as vocal chord control or even a demon throwing someone on the ground, may be caused by a demon without requiring internal habitation."[2] What if these authors are correct and all control is external? You could still have a believer rolling on the ground, speaking in demonic voices, in desperate need of help.

We believe the critical issue is how to help this person. To find freedom from the spiritual bondage, however you want to describe it, the believer must assume personal responsiblity to believe the truth of his or her identity in Christ, submit to God by repenting of sin, put on the spiritual armor and resist the devil. Regardless of where the demons are located, it is trusting God's truth and His truth alone that sets people free (see John 8:31,32). We have never cast demons out of anybody as some kind of "outside authority agent," and we don't teach others to do it. We simply encourage believers to exercise their responsibility to "submit therefore to God. Resist the devil" (James 4:7) using the kind, compassionate model described by Paul in 2 Timothy 2:24-26.

Through the years, we have had the privilege of helping thousands find their freedom in Christ, freedom from Satan's lies and freedom from their pasts. Many were in bondage to their past, others had deep sexual problems, eating disorders and other seemingly unmanageable behaviors. Few of these people knew who they were as children of God, and all struggled in their thought lives. I (Neil) have personally counseled hundreds of people who heard voices, and nearly every situation involved a spiritual battle for their minds. You may want to read *Released from Bondage*. It contains testimonies of Christians who were in bondage and their accounts of how they got out of it. You will read about the strong spiritual component in every single person's problems. How you choose to label the conflict is almost irrelevant to us. The fact that Christ was their answer and truth set them free is the real issue. And we, the Church, are the only hope these dear people have because the secular world does not believe they could possibly be having demonic problems.

Can we bind Satan?

We believe the answer is "yes" in the limited sense (we bind Satan by living responsible lives under the authority of Christ), but "no" in the generic sense. If we could completely bind Satan and render him inoperative on this planet, then the New Testament would instruct us to do so. At that point, we could preach the Gospel unhindered, and everyone would be free. But no such instruction exists in the Bible. Satan will only be bound by an angel under God's authority, and then he will be thrown into the pit and finally into the lake of fire at the final judgment (see Revelation 20). Presently, Satan is still the god of this world and the prince of power of the air.

Satan's forces, however, were defeated by Christ at the cross and are now subject to our authority when we stand in Christ and resist the devil (see Ephesians 6:10-20; Colossians 2:9-15). God has granted us the authority to "bind what shall be bound in heaven" (Matthew 16:19; 18:18). In other words, we have the spiritual capacity to discern God's will and then, confident in the finished work of Christ, proclaim it in the spiritual realm. We have authority over demons as long as we remain strong in the Lord and operate in His strength (see Ephesians 6:10). Our authority is not independent of Him. We have only the authority to do God's will. The moment we step out in the flesh and do our own thing we will probably get thrashed. The effectiveness of binding the strong man (see Matthew 12:29) is dependent upon the leading of the Holy Spirit and subject to the scope and limits of the written Word of God.

God has granted the Church this authority over Satan and his demons so that we can carry out the mission He has given us and proclaim the gospel worldwide (see Matthew 28:18-20). In fact, the Great Commission begins with the words, "'All authority has been given to Me in heaven and on earth. Go therefore and make disciples of all the nations'" (Matthew 28:18,19). Clearly, we have the authority we need over the enemy to continue the work of Christ and fulfill His commission to us. But even Jesus Himself did nothing on His own initiative; He did only that which came from His heavenly Father (see John 5:19, 30; 12:49). Likewise, only when we are submissive to the Lord's will do we have spiritual authority over the enemy (James 4:7).

When and how often should I pray to bind Satan?

Any answer to this question has to take into account the totality of Scripture. Romans 13:1-5 clearly teaches that all authority has been established by God, and 1 Corinthians 4:1-3 instructs us to be good stewards of all that God has entrusted to us. We cannot, however, commit something to the Lord that does not belong to us, nor are we to minister in violation of the command to be subject to all governing authorities. However, if you are in total submission and you have the legal right to be at a certain place for a specific time, then commit that time and place to the Lord. If you are in agreement about God's will, then pray together that the enemy be bound in that place, for that time and for the sake of ministry.

Can we bind demons over long distances?
Discernment and submission—not distance—are the critical issues in the spiritual realm. Prayers for the protection of missionaries, for instance, are very much appreciated and effective in the spiritual realm. Paul specifically asked for such prayers in Ephesians 6:18-20. These prayers should be offered in agreement with the missionaries in the field and they should be consistent with the laws of the land in which they minister.

Another note of caution: Praying for the binding of demonic activity in the life of a person who has yielded himself to the enemy may not be effective. Instead, at some point, that person must assume responsibility for his or her own freedom through faith in Christ. If he or she is under your spiritual authority (in the case of a child or a church member), God may lead you to stand against Satan in prayer and bind the enemy's influence until the person under your care turns to God in repentance and faith. But you can't find lasting freedom for that person apart from his or her personal decision to name Jesus Christ as Lord and Savior.

Why doesn't a demon leave when you pray in the name of Jesus?
God has delegated us all the authority we need to carry out the ministry assignment He has given us, but individual freedom is ultimately the result of personal repentance and faith in Christ. Simply using the name of Jesus as a formula for finding freedom accomplishes nothing unless we are in complete submission to Him. (See Acts 19:13-16 where the sons of Sceva learned this the hard way.)

But what if you have submitted to God and resisted the devil but still seem to be suffering from demonic oppression? First, God may allow Satan and his demons to harass believers for their own growth. We have two clear biblical examples in Job and Paul (see 2 Corinthians 12:7-10 where Paul is suffering at the hands of "a messenger of Satan"). God can and does use whatever means He wants to discipline us in order that we may share in His holiness. Second, God may be bringing you through a growth process in which you are gradually dealing with all the entrances of Satan into your life. I (Neil) refer to this as the onion effect. The Lord is peeling off one layer at a time. To do it all at once would be overwhelming for those who have suffered a lot of abuse.

Also, keep in mind that as long as we are in the world, we are subject to the attacks, temptations, accusations and deceptions of the evil one. God promises us His presence and protection (see John 17:15-19). Any suffering or pressure from the enemy that God allows (see 1 Corinthians 10:13) is intended for our growth and His glory. We must therefore always turn to God in humble submission, repentance and faith (see Romans 8:18-39).

Can Satan read my mind?

Satan cannot perfectly read your mind, but no single passage in Scripture states this definitively. We infer that Satan cannot read our minds for a number of reasons. First, Satan is a created being, originally a powerful angel (see Ezekiel 28:13,14). Though he aspired to be like God (see Isaiah 14:13,14), he is not God's equal in any way. Only God has the ability to be everywhere—all-present, all-knowing and all-powerful. Therefore, only God has complete and continual knowledge of our minds' activities (see Psalm 139).

Second, everywhere in the Bible that angels or demons interact with people or God, information must be exchanged through communication. Certainly if Satan could have read Jesus' mind, he would have altered his doomed strategy in the temptations he devised (see Matthew 4:1-11). Instead, the devil tries different temptations, and each time Jesus resists him verbally, using the sword of the Spirit as we are called to do (see Ephesians 6:17).

Third, in Daniel 2 King Nebuchadnezzar wisely demanded that his Chaldean sorcerers reveal the content of both of his dreams before interpreting them in order to validate the divine origin of the interpretation. The sorcerers were stumped because they knew their normal sources of power and information (demons) could not read the king's mind. Only God is the true revealer of such mysteries (see Daniel 2:11,22,28,29,47). Certainly, if Satan had been able to read the king's mind, he would have been able to keep Daniel from advancing in the king's service.

What Satan can affect, apparently, is one's thought processes through the flesh. He is, for instance, indicted for blinding the minds of the unbelieving (see 2 Corinthians 4:3,4), and he darkens their understanding (see Ephesians 2:1-3 and 4:17-19). He and his demons can communicate false doctrine (see 2 Corinthians 11:13-15; Galatians 1:8; 1 Timothy 4:1; 1 John 4:1-3) and his demons can impact the thoughts of believers as well. Satan is credited for prompting Ananias to lie to the Holy Spirit (see Acts 5:1-3), for moving David to consider his own strengths when he numbered the people of Israel (see 1 Chronicles 21:1,2), for inspiring Peter's resistance to Christ's statement about His impending death (see Matthew 16:23), for inspiring worldly wisdom rooted in jealousy and ambition (see James 3:14,15; 4:7), and for leading minds away from devotion to Christ (see 2 Corinthians 11:3). It isn't hard for Satan to know what you're thinking when he gives you the thoughts!

Furthermore, Satan and his demons use deception to give the impression they can read minds and know the future through divination and fortune-telling (see Acts 16:16,17). Satan has also had opportunities since the beginning of creation to observe human behavior. As a result, he has a thorough working knowledge of human behavior. He has learned what he must do to derive certain behaviors from the person he attacks. He can also influence events by influencing key leaders. He uses this deception to give the impression he is like God, able to read minds and control the future. But remember that Christ has triumphed over Satan and, in Christ, you have the responsibility to resist him in submission to God. When you do, he will flee (see Colossians 3:15; James 4:7).

Is Satan as powerful as God?

To the person who is under severe attack by the devil and who does not understand the character of God, Satan can seem extremely powerful. At times, a person may even be tempted to believe the lie that the devil is God's equal in power, but nothing could be further from the truth!

Satan is a created being and, like all of God's creatures, is subject to the final authority of God. Satan is not permitted to do anything unless God first allows him. In Job 1 and 2, God granted permission for the devil to touch Job's possessions and even his physical body, but refused to allow Satan to kill him. And, shortly before He went to the cross, Jesus warns Peter that "Satan has demanded permission to sift [him] like wheat" (Luke 22:31) and tells Peter that He is praying that his faith will be strong. Clearly, Satan is bound by the authoritative decrees of Almighty God. The devil has to ask God for permission before acting; he does not have equal authority with God.

Neither does Satan have God's great wisdom. God's understanding is infinite (see Psalm 147:5) whereas Satan's is limited. The devil, for instance, obviously did not understand that the death of Christ on the cross would soon be followed by His triumphant resurrection, His ascension to glory and the giving of the Holy Spirit to empower all believers. If he had known all that, he would never had conspired to put Him to death (see 1 Corinthians 2:8)! Furthermore, the Bible teaches that "nothing in all creation is hidden from God's sight" (Hebrews 4:13, NIV). Only God "knows the secrets of the heart" (Psalm 44:21, *NIV*), and Satan is unable to perfectly read our minds.

As you begin to better understand who God really is and who you are in Christ, you will see that you have no need to fear Satan's power. He is a defeated foe, and in Christ you have all the authority you need to discern his schemes and resist him (see Colossians 2:8-15; James 4:7).

Why does God let Satan have so much power?

This question, in a variety of forms, has perplexed human beings for centuries. Many people have expressed it this way: "If God is so good, why is there so much evil and suffering in the world?" or "If God is so powerful, why doesn't He simply put an end to all the wickedness and pain in the world?" To be sure, our efforts to understand this issue fall short of a complete answer, and to a certain extent it will remain a mystery to us this side of heaven.

We do know, however, that God is the Author of life, not death. He created Lucifer. Lucifer became Satan by his own rebellion (see Isaiah 14; Ezekiel 28). He then instigated the rebellion of one-third of the angels who became demons (see Revelation 12). God created Adam who rebelled by sinning and led a parade of fallen humanity. Sin in the world is the result of God's creation rebelling against Him. The Lord, however, remains both all powerful and completely good (see Jude 25; Exodus 34:6). Therefore, at any time, He could choose to say, "Enough is enough" and put a stop to all the activities of Satan as well as to all the activities of us sinful people—and one day He will. Until that Second Coming of Christ, however, we face the harsh reality that incredible evil and suffering abound in our world.

Does God see? Does God care? We answer both troubling questions with a resounding, "Yes!" The Lord Jesus, when He walked on the earth, wept at the grave of His dear friend Lazarus (see John 11:35). At another time, "Seeing the multitudes, He felt compassion for them, because they were distressed and downcast like sheep without a shepherd" (Matthew 9:36). These are certainly not the emotions and reactions of a distant or aloof God!

"Why then," you may ask, "doesn't this omnipotent God respond with compassion for all who suffer today?" The answer to that question is "He already has!" The Lord Jesus Christ did not choose to remain on His lofty throne in heaven, far above the pain and misery that Satan causes in this world. Instead, He came to earth clothed in human flesh. He took everything Satan could throw at Him and never gave up or gave in. Jesus even died an excruciating death on the cross to pay for our evil, so that one day we will spend eternity in paradise with Him (see Philippians 2:5-11)! Jesus defeated Satan at the cross and sealed his doom forever. Judgment has already been passed on to the devil; one day he will begin to serve his eternal sentence.

"But it seems to be taking so long for Jesus to come back," you say. Perhaps to us it seems like God is taking His good old time, but God is right on schedule. Listen to the words of the apostle Peter: "The Lord is not slow in keeping his promise [to come again], as some understand slowness. He is patient with you, not wanting anyone to perish, but everyone to come to repentance" (2 Peter 3:9, *NIV*).

God is waiting for people like you and me to turn from our sin and put our faith in Christ. It is out of His kindness that He waits to put an end to the devil's power on earth. For when God puts His foot down and says, "Enough!" to Satan, He will do the same with sinful men and women, and that will be the end of history as we know it. Christ will return, judgment will come, and those who have not believed in Him will be doomed with the devil to the lake of fire (see Revelation 20:10-15).

In the meantime, God has given us the tremendous privilege and responsibility of proclaiming the good news of salvation to the people around us who have yet to respond. We can do a lot to lessen the power of Satan in people's lives by winning them to Christ and helping them become strong in their identity as a child of God. The Holy Spirit gives us the power to make disciples for Christ as we depend on Him.

So we can sit around cursing the darkness, or we can light a candle. But rather than spending our time bemoaning the fact that Satan seems to have so much power, let us be about our Father's business of building His Church. The gates of hell will not prevail against us (see Matthew 16:18)! And someday every tear will be wiped away, and the universe will be eradicated of evil (see Revelation 21:4).

Do I need to get rid of crystal jewelry?
The fact that some practitioners of New Age thinking have adopted crystals as objects through which evil can manifest its power does not make crystals themselves evil. God has created all things for us to enjoy, and crystal can make beautiful jewelry (see 1 Timothy 6:17). Many believers see the beauty and order of crystals pointing to a beautiful God who created the universe with a marvelous order.

If, however, you have been using crystals as "power objects," it may be advisable for you to follow the practice of the Ephesian believers in Acts 19:18-20 and remove any bridges the enemy could use to get back into your life. If you are unsure about what to do, simply ask God for wisdom, determining ahead of time that you will trust His guidance as He makes His will for you clear (see James 1:5-8).

GOD, CHRIST, AND THE LIFE OF FAITH
Where was God when I was being abused?
God was there, and He was greatly grieved over what happened. Psalm 94 assures us that God indeed does see all forms of abuse and oppression and that He is a God of vengeance and justice. He is also our help, our stronghold, and our refuge. Rather than focus on what God didn't do in his life (that is, stop the abuse in your life), the psalmist focuses on his relationship with God, confident that God will one day mete out perfect justice.

It may also help to remember that God made human beings with the responsibility to choose—even to choose to disobey Him. God does not now change that freedom and prevent people from choosing to do evil. Besides, to take away our choice would be to remove the possibility of us choosing to trust God.

In light of the pain we experience at the hands of others, our confidence and hope lies in the truth that God is able to bring healing and that He even uses the pain to build strength of character—a Christlike character—in us. We cannot guarantee that you will escape evil in this sick and fallen world (see John 16:33), but we can reassure you that you don't have to be a perpetual victim of your past. In Christ, God has provided us with a way to overcome our past, and we have to assume our responsibility to choose that path of freedom.

One more important word about suffering comes from Job, a book which teaches us how to deal with the loss and pain that comes our way in this world. As his suffering progresses, Job never gives up on his relationship with God. He argues, he expresses his deep disappointments, and he even asks God for a trial and the opportunity to plead his case about God's apparent injustice (see Job 9,10). Through all his trials, Job never gives up on God: "Though he slay me, yet will I trust in him: but I will maintain mine own ways before him" (Job 13:15, *KJV*). The key is to be honest about your deep disappointments with God and allow Him to speak to you (see Job 38-41).

Don't suffer in denial. Let God know about your anger and disappointment with Him. Then you will be able to see God and yourself clearly enough to follow Job's example and repent of your wrong expectations of God (see Job 42:1-6). Keep in mind, too, that Job's latter state was more blessed than his former state. God never told Job why he was suffering, but God used suffering to increase Job's trust in Him and to bless Job. Romans 8:18-39 assures us that God's plan for our glory includes suffering, but this suffering can never separate us from His love for us as demonstrated in Christ Jesus' death on the cross.

What does "acquiescence" mean—or why can't we passively live victoriously in Christ?

According to the dictionary, the word "acquiesce" means "to agree or consent quietly without protest." In our Christian life, acquiescence means spiritual passivity, and to live passively is to accept defeat by default. Spiritual freedom, however, can only be found when we actively make a series of choices based on the truth of God's Word. For example, we were all born spiritually dead and separated from God because of Adam's sin (see Romans 5:12-15; Ephesians 2:1-3). When we were born again, we became new creations in Christ. But our minds were not instantly reprogrammed, and many of our old habits are still with us. Now that we are alive in Christ, you and I can be transformed by the renewing of our minds (see Romans 12:2). That renewal won't happen, however, unless you are "diligent to present yourself approved to God as a workman who does not need to be ashamed, handling accurately the word of truth" (2 Timothy 2:15). Spiritual victory is realized as we actively choose to place our faith or trust in Jesus Christ for justification and sanctification, rejecting dead works and other false means (see Romans 5:1; Ephesians 2:4-9).

Dealing with intergenerational and corporate sin also calls for an active faith. For that reason, in Step Seven, "Acquiescence versus Renunciation," we take an active stand by faith against any sins of our ancestors that may result in spiritual problems in our lives today (see Exodus 20:4-6). It is important to understand that we are not guilty for our parents' sins, but that because they sinned we are likely to suffer the consequences. Some people struggle to accept the fact that sin can have intergenerational consequences even though one of the most well-accepted phenomenon of our day is the fact that the cycle of abuse continues in families from one generation to the next. The wonderful truth is that we can stop that cycle of abuse if we actively take our place in Christ.

Some people might explain the transmission of sin environmentally and genetically but not spiritually. But Jeremiah 32:16-18 says that iniquity is passed on into the bosom of the next generation, a statement which negates the role of the environment. The argument that iniquity is passed on genetically doesn't fit with the definition of iniquity. (Iniquity refers to self-rule or self-will which operates from an independent spirit.) The issue is also a spiritual one, and we therefore need to actively choose to confess and renounce all the sins of our ancestors so that we may find the freedom God promises (see Leviticus 26:38-40 and Ezekiel 18:18-22). If, like the kings which followed Jereboam, we simply continue in the sins of our ancestors, the spiritual bondage will continue.

Hear God's admonition to actively assume responsibility for our minds and actively resist the devil: "Therefore, gird your minds for action, keep sober in spirit.... Be on the alert. Your adversary, the devil, prowls about like a roaring lion, seeking someone to devour. But resist him, firm in your faith" (1 Peter 1:13; 5:8,9). Even the armor of God requires active participation on our part: "Therefore, take up the full armor of God, that you may be able to resist in the evil day, and having done everything, to stand firm. Stand firm therefore..." (Ephesians 6:13,14). A passive faith just doesn't work.

Why do I have to worry about sin if Christ has already died for my sins?
If you have confessed your sin and named Jesus as your Savior and Lord, you don't have to worry about your sin. When Christ died on the cross, He paid the penalty for all of our sins—past, present and future. Therefore, as Paul teaches, "there is therefore now no condemnation for those who are in Christ Jesus" (Romans 8:1). The apostle also writes, "Blessed are they whose transgressions are forgiven, whose sins are covered" (Romans 4:7, *NIV*). We are forgiven; we are assured of having eternal life. Those are matters we don't have to worry about.

Although God has committed Himself to not condemn us for our sin, Satan has not made that promise. Satan is an accuser (see Revelation 12:10). His purpose is to try to place us under guilt and condemnation for sins which God has totally forgiven. He torments believers with thoughts like, "God can never really forgive me for this" and "You might as well give up. You'll never be free from this sin. So why bother asking for forgiveness again?" If we believe lies like these, we will live in bondage and not the freedom that Christ has purchased and provided for us.

So don't worry about your sin in reference to eternal life. Rejoice in the forgiveness God has provided through the death of His Son Jesus on the cross. At the same time, commit yourself to living a righteous life. Paul asked, "Are we to continue to sin that grace might increase? May it never be! How shall we who died to sin still live in it?" (Romans 6:1,2). You should confess any and all sin which the Holy Spirit makes you aware of. To confess is to agree with God that what He says about our sinfulness is true (see 1 John 1:5–2:2). You don't need to ask for forgiveness since you are already forgiven—but you do need to acknowledge your sin and consider yourself alive in Christ and dead to sin (see Romans 6:11). Besides, why would you want to go back into the bondage of sin when you can be alive and free in Christ? Choose to submit to God and to resist the devil (see James 4:7) and renounce any effort on the enemy's part to place you under guilt and condemnation.

Your responsibility is to walk by faith in God and His truth, relying on the power of the Holy Spirit, and you will not carry out the desire of the flesh (see Galatians 5:16). You walk by faith when you choose to believe what God has done for you in Christ and what it means to be His child. We strongly recommend that you read *Living Free in Christ*, which explains the truth about who you are in Christ and how He meets your deepest needs.

If we are now saints, do we no longer struggle with our old sin nature? This question may be prompted by the confusion that arises from the difference between interpretive terminology and biblical terminology. The term "old sin nature" does not occur in the Bible. It is an interpretive term used at times to explain two biblical terms, "the old man" (*ho palaion anthropon*) and "the flesh" (*sarx*). Unfortunately, the term "old sin nature" has been used almost interchangeably for both these terms, leaving the impression that after salvation occurs, nothing essential about the believer's relationship to sin has changed.

The Bible, however, teaches otherwise. It separates the two concepts "the old man" and "the flesh" rather dramatically. Consistently, "the old man" refers to something that was crucified or put off at salvation. Note the use of the aorist tense in the verses listed below. (The Greek aorist tense denotes the simple occurrence of an action without reference to its completeness, duration or repetition.[3])

- "Knowing this, that our old man is crucified [aorist tense] with

[Jesus], that the body of sin might be destroyed, that henceforth we should not serve sin" (Romans 6:6, *KJV*).

- "That you put off, [aorist tense] concerning your former conduct, the old man which grows corrupt according to the deceitful lusts" (Ephesians 4:22, *NKJV*).
- "Lie not one to another, seeing that [you] have put off [aorist tense] the old man with his deeds" (Colossians 3:9, *KJV*).

Now consider how the biblical word for "nature" (*phusis*) is used to describe the change that takes place at the moment of salvation:

- "Among whom also we all once conducted ourselves in the lusts of our flesh, fulfilling the desires of the flesh and of the mind, and were by nature children of wrath, just as the others" (Ephesians 2:3, *NKJV*).
- "Whereby are given unto us exceeding great and precious promises: that by these [you] might be partakers of the divine nature, having escaped the corruption that is in the world through lust" (2 Peter 1:4, *KJV*).

The Bible describes an exchange of natures (*phusis*) rather than the addition of natures. One nature has died; a new one has replaced it.

Nevertheless, using the term "flesh" (*sarx*), the Bible describes the source of our ongoing struggle with sin despite our new identity. The New International Version has translated the Greek word *sarx* with the interpretive phrase "sinful nature" in many key passages which indicate that believers can and do struggle with the flesh (i.e., Romans 7:18; 8:2-9; Galatians 5:16-24).

So, to answer the original question, if you mean "the flesh" when you use the term "sinful nature," we believe in the ongoing struggle of the believer with sin through the flesh. John indicates that believers who deny that they are struggling with sin are living in complete deception (see 1 John 1:5-10). Much of our ministry therefore involves bringing secret and unresolved sin to light so it can be confessed and cleansing can be received.

We also believe, however, that the Bible clearly teaches that something essential in the believer's relationship with sin has changed at a core level and that this change is talked about in the biblical terms "old man" or "nature" and addressed in the concept that we are a new creation in Christ (see 2 Corinthians 5:17). Consider the following passages that contrast who we were in Adam (see 1 Corinthians 15:22) with who we are now in Christ:

Old Man (Col. 3:9)	By Ancestry	New Man (Col. 3:10)
Children of Wrath (Eph. 2:1-3)	By Nature	Partaker of Divine Nature (2Pet. 1:4)
In the Flesh (Rom. 8:8)	By Birth	In the Spirit (Rom. 8:9)
Walk After the Flesh By Choice (Rom. 8:12,13)		Walk After the Spirit (Gal. 5:16)

So is it proper to describe ourselves as "saints who sin" rather than "sinners" if we still struggle with the flesh? Again, popular terminology is a little confusing. "I'm just a sinner saved by grace" has been used at times to express humility before God, and humbling ourselves before God is good. But this phrase has also been used to rationalize the absence of victory over sin, which isn't good.

A quick survey of the Bible yields much strong support for the view that God wants believers to see themselves as saints. In the King James Version, believers are called "saints," "holy ones," or "righteous ones" more than 240 times. In contrast, unbelievers are called "sinners" over 330 times. Clearly, the term "sinner" is normally used to refer to an unbeliever and the term "saint" to a believer. Only three possible exceptions are found—1 Timothy 1:15; James 4:8; James 5:20. Even if all these three uses of the word "sinner" refer to believers, only one could possibly refer to a mature believer's humble perspective of himself as a "sinner" (an interpretation of the use of the present tense in 1 Timothy 1:15 that is open to debate based on the contextual fact that Paul is looking back on his conversion). The passages in James refer either to believers functioning like "sinners" in bondage to sin or to unbelievers who have not yet experienced faith in Christ.

In conclusion, by a ratio of at least 240 to 1, the biblical emphasis is to view ourselves as saints, saved by the grace of God, who still struggle with sin in the flesh. By a ratio of at least 330 to 3, "sinner" would be the normal biblical designation for an unbeliever. In using our material, it doesn't matter if you still prefer to think of believers as having two competing natures (old nature and new nature) as long as your view of our new identity in Christ corresponds to the biblical view of the real power and victory this identity can give us over sin. We think believers will experience greater victory if they trust the biblical view of themselves as saints who are "dead to sin but alive to God in Christ Jesus" and who therefore now have the power to choose to live according to their new Master, Jesus Christ (see Romans 6:1-14; 8:1-17).

SIN, CONFESSION AND FORGIVENESS
Why should I confess in front of another person when God can hear me? Why should I say things out loud?
James 4:7 says, "Submit therefore to God. Resist the devil and he will flee from you." We submit to God when we confess our sin to God, and when we do so, He forgives and cleanses us (see 1 John 1:9). And, because God is omniscient and knows our thoughts (see Psalm 139), we are assured that He hears us even when we silently confess our sins to Him. With such confession, we have submitted to God, but have we resisted the devil? We have received forgiveness, but have we found freedom? In our ministry, we have seen how verbally confessing sin and thereby resisting the devil helps many people find freedom. Why is this the case?

In many New Testament examples, the confrontation between believers and Satan and his evil associates is verbal (see Matthew 4:10 and 17:18; Mark 5:2-8; Luke 9:42; Revelation 12:10,11). In fact, in Ephesians 6:10-17 we are told to resist the devil using the Word (Greek = *rhema*) of God. "Rhema" normally indicates the spoken word of God or God's Word applied specifically (see Matthew 4:4; 18:16; Acts 5:20; Romans 10:17,18). Believers at Ephesus applied this principle of verbal confession in Acts 19:18-20 when they publicly disclosed their participation in cultic and occult practices. Clearly they were concerned about any doors they may have left open to the demonic (see Acts 19:11-17). The Greek word for "confess" in Acts 19:18 usually indicates a verbal confession (see Mark 1:5; Romans 14:11). Such verbal confession seems to be a way to "submit to God and resist the devil" at the same time.

Note, too, the teaching of James 5:13-20, the most definitive instruction to individuals and to the Church about what to do for those who are sick and suffering. Apparently, their problem has a spiritual dimension (verses 15, 16, 19 and 20 all focus on the spiritual dimension of their sickness and suffering). Therefore the person who is suffering is instructed to pray (v. 13), seek prayer from his spiritual leaders (vv. 14,15), confess sins (the same word for public confession used in Acts 19:18), and turn back to the truth of God (vv. 19,20). The result is described as "healing" (v. 16), from a Greek word that can indicate either physical healing (as in Matthew 8:8; 15:28; Mark 5:25) or spiritual freedom from demonic oppression (as in Luke 9:42; Acts 10:38). Though forgiveness is obtained through confession to God, verbal confession and agreement in prayer may be critical in finding spiritual freedom and healing.

On a practical level, many people have found it very freeing to share their secret sins with another believer and then experience acceptance and unconditional love instead of the rejection they have feared all their lives. For many people, this moment of experiencing God's unconditional love through His children is the starting point of learning to trust God and other people at a more fundamental level. In other words, verbal confession can be a step into the light. The apostle John identifies two important results of learning to stop hiding in darkness and beginning to walk in the light: "If we walk in the light as He Himself is in the light, we have fellowship with one another, and the blood of Jesus His son cleanses us from all sin" (1 John 1:7).

Can I forgive if I don't feel like it?

You not only can, but you must! Forgiveness is one of the most important steps toward freedom in Christ. Jesus Himself predicates God's forgiveness of us on our forgiveness of others: "And forgive us our debts, as we also have forgiven our debtors.... For if you forgive men for their transgressions, your heavenly Father will also forgive you. But if you do not forgive men, then your Father will not forgive your transgressions" (Matthew 6:12,14,15). The apostle Paul teaches us that unresolved anger gives the devil a place in our lives and calls us to "be kind and compassionate to one another, forgiving each other, just as in Christ God forgave you" (Ephesians 4:26,27,32, *NIV*).

The question above addresses the relationship between feelings and forgiveness. Realize that if God commands us to do so, we can forgive whether or not we feel like forgiving. We don't always feel like going to church, praying or studying the Bible, but we choose to do these things anyway because they are necessary for our growth. Our feelings change as we obey God and enter into His presence. Similarly, forgiveness is a choice—an act of the will—that begins a process of emotional healing and the restoration of our relationships with God. Don't wait for the emotions to heal or lead the way before you obey God and choose to forgive.

We must also forgive from the heart if we are to experience the freedom of forgiveness (see Matthew 18:34,35). It is not the words we say that accomplish forgiveness. It is facing the hurt and the hatred and then choosing to forgive from the heart. Such emotional honesty is absolutely necessary as we choose to forgive, and this is where many evangelicals stumble. They never admit their anger and simply forgive from the head, trying to keep the painful memories out of their minds.

Forgiveness, then, is something you can do regardless of what you are feeling. It is a decision that you can and must make in obedience to God and for your own sake. Go as deep as you can with your emotions because that is where the healing is going to take place. Don't be afraid to face the hurt and the hate. Instead, trust the Lord to bring to the surface whatever painful emotions you need to deal with and then trust Him to help you deal with them as well.

A good way to do that is to name the offense you are forgiving and to describe how that offense made you feel about yourself (rejected, unwanted, unloved, dirty or something similar). Now that you're again feeling this pain, hurt or anger, choose to let the debt go and agree to live with the consequences of the sin. Although the situation isn't fair, you have no choice but to deal with the effects of that person's sin. More accurately, the only real choice you have is whether to deal with the consequences of another person's sin against you in the bondage of bitterness, or in the freedom of forgiveness.

Why should I forgive someone who hasn't repented of his or her sin? Won't doing so just lead to more abuse?
Nowhere do we teach that forgiveness means tolerating sin of any kind, especially abuse. Forgiveness does not mean staying in an abusive situation and giving the perpetrator more opportunities to inflict damage. The loving thing to do is to confront abuse and help the perpetrators acknowledge and accept their responsibility.

At this point, you might find it helpful to understand that forgiveness and reconciliation are separate issues. Forgiveness is necessary even when reconciliation may not be possible. In many situations, emotional healing from bitterness, hatred and anger is necessary, but reconciliation is impossible or inadvisable. A person who was abused by a now deceased parent, for instance, will never find healing by waiting for the offender to repent. That person can't, and many other people won't. The deceased abuser has already met his or her Maker and Judge, and hanging on to bitterness and hatred won't help you or impact that person. Also, a person who was ritually abused needs to find emotional healing but should never be reconciled with the perpetrators. Simply put, forgiving is releasing a debt. It is agreeing to live with the consequences of another person's sin and relinquishing the right to seek revenge which God assures us is His domain (see Romans 12:17-21).

Some believers, however, have used Luke 17:3,4 to teach that we should not forgive unless repentance occurs:

> "Be on your guard! If your brother sins, rebuke him; and if he repents, forgive him. And if he sins against you seven times a day, and returns to you seven times, saying, 'I repent,' forgive him."

This passage focuses on forgiveness in the context of reconciling a relationship in which we are called to rebuke sin and help bring others to repentance. It doesn't specifically say that we shouldn't forgive if they don't repent (even though this may be implied). Furthermore, we are not called to play the role of the Holy Spirit, rebuking every sin in every person we meet. Honesty about sin is necessary for genuine reconciliation, and there is a time to refuse a cheap reconciliation without repentance. But note that Christ's main point here is not about withholding forgiveness but extending it, even repeatedly, to someone who is struggling in the relationship. We are to be grace-givers, not repentance-demanders.

As we take people through the Steps to Freedom, we find that people who wait for another's repentance are locked in bitterness toward literally dozens of people. Many are still bitter about an old boyfriend who jilted them or a boss who passed them over for a promotion. We see little gained by hanging on to bitterness and somehow trying to exact repentance and force reconciliation. Our freedom cannot be dependent upon whether another person will repent.

In the Steps, we deal primarily with the volitional and emotional side of forgiveness as it relates directly to our relationship with God. Jesus says, "Whenever you stand praying, forgive, if you have anything against anyone; so that your Father also who is in heaven may forgive you your transgressions" (Mark 11:25). Here, forgiveness is not portrayed as some long, drawn-out reconciliation process. It can be done while you stand in prayer. Nor is forgiveness shown to be conditional, extended only to some people for some transgressions. Instead, forgiveness is pictured as part of our normal prayer life, it is extended to anyone for anything, and it may or may not be a prelude to reconciliation. Furthermore, forgiveness on a human level is necessary if we are to experience forgiveness from God (see Matthew 6:12,14,15). Forgiveness is also a crucial element in resolving anger and bitterness (see Ephesians 4:27,32). Only when we are free from bitterness can we pursue reconciliation from a biblical perspective and a godly attitude.

Must I seek forgiveness and reconciliation from those I have hurt in order to find freedom?
Matthew 5:23,24 gives us guidance on this point:

> "If therefore you are presenting your offering at the altar, and there remember that your brother has something against you, leave your offering there before the altar, and go your way; first be reconciled to your brother, and then come and present your offering."

Christ is teaching that God will bring to mind those situations which may be hindering our worship of Him and therefore need to be dealt with. We are to take responsibility and deal quickly with people who are clearly aware that we have wronged them. (This does not include mental sins of which others may be unaware [i.e., asking someone to forgive you for lusting after him or her will only damage and confuse the relationship].) The goal is to work for reconciliation (see Romans 12:18) by clearly owning up to your sin, labeling it as wrong, offering no excuses and seeking forgiveness. In general, you should take these steps in person and not through a letter, which can be easily misunderstood or fall into the wrong hands.

Is it right to forgive God?
Technically, no. God cannot do anything wrong. But you had better deal with your bitterness and anger toward God if you want to find spiritual freedom. Again, since we are dealing with the volitional and emotional dimension of forgiveness in the Steps to Freedom, we often process these feelings toward God in the forgiveness step. What we are actually doing is being honest about the disappointment and pain we feel in our relationship to God and repenting of our false expectations and wrong attitudes toward God. Though Job clung to God throughout his ordeal and was emotionally honest with Him all along, the breakthrough for him

came with repenting of his demanding spirit and letting God be God (see Job 42:1-6). We try not to get too hung up on exactly how someone expresses this repentance. We're sure God forgives someone whose heart is right, but who says, "God, I forgive you for...". Whenever possible, we encourage people to use the correct terminology, but the attitude of the heart is the critical issue.

Isn't forgiving yourself like playing God?

Again we are dealing with anger that stems from false expectations, in this case, false expectations for ourselves. In answer to the question, when we forgive ourselves, we are simply accepting and agreeing with God's forgiveness of us. Many people, however, find it easier to connect with their self-directed anger by saying, "I forgive myself for...". Often people mentally beat themselves up for sins God has already forgiven. Playing judge, jury and warden in your own life like this is more like playing God than choosing to affirm His forgiveness.

Isn't it selfish to forgive for our sakes?

Throughout the Bible, obedience brings blessing and disobedience brings cursing or negative consequences. After laying out the choice between the blessed life of obedience and the cursed life of disobedience (see Deuteronomy 27:1-3014), God asks Israel to choose life instead of judgment (see vv. 30:19,20). Is it selfish for Israel to obey God and choose to enjoy His blessings and avoid His discipline? Hardly. Neither is it selfish to choose to forgive in order to escape emotional torment (see Matthew 18:34,35), to have our prayers unhindered (see Mark 11:25), to thwart Satan's schemes against the Church (see 2 Corinthians 2:10,11), to remove Satan's place in our lives (see Ephesians 4:27,32), or to enjoy God's forgiveness (see Matthew 6:14,15). What higher motive or greater benefit could we have for forgiving than the restoration of our relationship with God? Certainly restoring your relationship with God cannot be considered a selfish motivation.

Can a Christian commit the "unpardonable sin"?

> "Therefore I say to you, any sin and blasphemy shall be forgiven men, but blasphemy against the Spirit shall not be forgiven. And whoever shall speak a word against the Son of

Man, it shall be forgiven him; but whoever shall speak
against the Holy Spirit, it shall not be forgiven him, either in
this age, or in the age to come" (Matthew 12:31,32).

At one point in His ministry, the Pharisees accused Jesus of performing
His miracles by the power of Beelzebul, a ruling territorial spirit. In
response, Jesus said that if He were casting out demons by the power of
Beelzebul, then Satan would be casting out Satan. Satan would be divided against himself, and his kingdom could not stand. Jesus then explained
that, since He was casting out demons by the Spirit of God, the kingdom
of God had come upon them (see Matthew 12:28). Clearly, they were
rejecting the Spirit of God by crediting His work to Beelzebul.

So why did Jesus say that a person can speak against Him, but not the
Holy Spirit? The answer to this question comes with understanding that
the unique role of the Holy Spirit was and is to give evidence to the work
of Christ and to lead us into all truth (see John 14:17-19; 16:7-15). The
only unpardonable sin is the sin of unbelief. If we refuse to accept the testimony given to us by the Holy Spirit, fight off His conviction of our sin,
and never accept the truth, we will never come to Christ for salvation. In
Christ, all our sins are forgiven. Therefore, no Christian can commit the
unpardonable sin. Only an unregenerate person who refuses to come to
Christ will die in his or her sins.

The accuser of the brethren, however, will often try to convince
Christians that they have committed the unpardonable sin so that they
will live in defeat. We encourage you to read *Living Free in Christ*, which was
written to help Christians understand their relationship with God and
their identity in Christ so that they can stand against such lies of our
adversary. Even as Christians, however, we can quench the Spirit. If we
do, we will impede the work of God and live a less than victorious life,
but we will not lose our salvation.

PSYCHOLOGY
**When you talk about counseling, what do you mean by the "theory of
integration"?**
In *Helping Others Find Freedom in Christ*, we spend the first five chapters
explaining our view of how to biblically help other people find spiritual
victory. Please read this material very carefully before forming an opinion
about what we teach regarding counseling and Christian counseling.

In answer to the question, let us say briefly that the theory of integration looks at the relationship between psychological research (Christian and secular) and biblical information about people, problems, and solutions. We do *not* believe that you can take equal input from psychological theory and research and from biblical data and arrive at "biblical counseling." The Bible is the authoritative source and must be foundational to our view of people, problems and solutions. We must carefully develop a biblical worldview from which to evaluate all data and every approach to helping others.

At the same time, we do *not* believe that all research is inherently evil and anti-biblical. After all, every pastor relies on historical and geographical data gathered by people who do not believe in the miracles of the Bible. We use their data about possible routes of the Exodus and the geography of Sinai, but—unlike them—we nevertheless believe in the reality of the parting of the Red Sea and the drowning of the Egyptians and the Almighty God who was and is active in human history.

Unlike history and geography, psychology and sociology are not precise sciences. What researchers in these fields have observed is helpful in describing what is, but it is not helpful in determining what should be. For example, the Bible clearly teaches that sin is perpetuated through the world (environmental factors), the flesh (internal factors), and the devil (spiritual factors) (see Ephesians 2:1-3). We have found that defense mechanisms identified in psychological research (denial, fantasy, emotional insulation, displacement, etc.) are useful descriptions of how Satan has deceived us, programming our flesh to respond in sinful, self-protective ways to environmental factors (the world). The solution to these defense mechanisms, however, is not found in psychology. These false ways of coping with life must be repented of and replaced with trust in God and His truth. Only then can we let go of the defense mechanisms because then, having found freedom in Christ, we won't need them.

A brief postscript: Psalm 19 describes the relative value of both natural and special revelation. Only special revelation—God's written Word—can guide us to victory over sin and our relationship with God, but natural revelation (in general, what we see in nature; in this discussion, psychology) can give us insight into God and the world He has created. The critical factor is developing a thoroughly biblical worldview as a frame of reference.

THE STEPS TO FREEDOM

Just saying a prayer at each Step to Freedom isn't going to make me free, is it?

Merely reading words out loud without any heartfelt affirmation can indeed be ineffective prayer. The purpose of the prayers suggested in the Steps to Freedom is to help focus on the important areas of truth found in the Scriptures. They are not magical formulas with power that is released if they are properly spoken. These prayers are only effective to the extent that they are sincerely offered to a powerful and loving God.

Remember that the Psalms are songs and prayers recorded by David and others to be read and sung in personal and public worship. Israel used the words of Deuteronomy 6:4-9 (the *shema*) as a daily prayer to remind themselves of the greatest commandment: "'love the Lord your God with all your heart, and with all your soul, and with all your mind'" (Matthew 22:37). But Jesus condemns the meaningless repetition of prayer formulas (characteristic of pagan worship) and offers a model for His followers (see Matthew 6:7-14).

Christ's intent in the Lord's Prayer is the same as ours in the Steps to Freedom: to give a guide that helps people focus on important aspects of prayer. We have found that some people who are caught in spiritual conflict need help focusing their attention in prayer. When people are having trouble connecting with God as they read the prayers, we suggest that they read the prayers through silently before reading them aloud. They can also read them more slowly if that helps them affirm in their heart what they are saying with their mouth.

One more note: If people knew how to get out of bondage, they would have gotten out a long time ago. Nobody likes living in bondage. But people need a very clear road map out of bondage, and that is what we intend the Steps to Freedom to provide. We have learned the hard way that people don't know how or what to pray for (see Romans 8:26). Of course the prayers themselves don't set you free. They are a guide for seeking the Lord who can and will set you free if you respond appropriately by faith and repentance. The Bible assures us that "the eyes of the LORD move to and fro throughout the earth that He may strongly support those whose heart is completely His" (2 Chronicles 16:9).

If my friend or family member calls you, can someone take him or her through the Steps to Freedom?

Freedom in Christ Ministries exists for the purpose of equipping churches, mission groups and other ministries to help people find their freedom in Christ. We are primarily a resource, training and equipping ministry—not a counseling service—for a very good reason. We believe that God has given the Church the responsibility of helping people find their freedom in Christ and bringing them to spiritual maturity. Too often these days, churches are relying on paid professionals to do spiritual work that can and should be done by trained laypeople. In fact, the vast majority of people worldwide who are being led through the Steps to Freedom are being led by equipped laypeople. Long range, we will help many more people by helping others learn how to take people through the steps rather than by doing it all ourselves.

When people contact our office, we try to refer them to someone in their area who can take them through the steps. Usually an appropriate counselor/encourager can be found. Sometimes our staff does make freedom appointments if they are training others as part of the training program, and we will try at times to provide some guidance over the phone. But we cannot directly help all those who are hurting, or we would neglect our call to equip others.

Sometimes a concerned friend or family member contacts us on behalf of someone else who is struggling. Although we are sensitive to such needs, we do not think it beneficial to encourage the person calling to seek our help for the friend or family member's particular difficulty. Rather, we feel it is best for the helping individual to direct the afflicted person to take personal responsibility for seeking out resources to help him or herself.

The best thing you can do if you want to help others, or if you yourself are struggling, is to seek to establish a freedom ministry in your local church. That's what this book is all about.

Notes

1. Fritz Rienecker and Cleon Rogers, *The Linguistic Key to the Greek New Testament* (Grand Rapids, Mich.: Zondervan, 1976, 1982 edition).
2. Thomas Ice and Robert Dean, *Overrun by Demons*, (Eugene, Ore.: Harvest House, 1990), pp. 127-128.
3. The Greek aorist tense is a special type of past tense. It conveys the meaning that an event happened at a specific time in the past and that the action was completed at that time. The Greek aorist is different from an imperfect past tense which conveys the meaning of an action that was begun in the past but continues to happen in the present.

A GLOSSARY OF RELIGIOUS, OCCULT, AND PSYCHOLOGICAL TERMS

The following list of terms is not exhaustive and is intended to be purely informational. By including some of the phenomena, we are not implying that we believe in their actual existence. Furthermore, many of the definitions are written from the perspective of those who believe in such practices and do not represent a biblical interpretation or evaluation of such occult practices or psychological categories. The primary source of each definition is indicated by the first number and the page number by the second number (1:400 means McDowell and Stewart's *Handbook of Today's Religions*, page 400).

SOURCES:

1. Josh McDowell and Don Stewart, *Handbook of Today's Religion* (San Bernardino, CA: Here's Life Publishing, 1983).
2. Nevil Drury, *Dictionary of Mysticism and the Occult* (New York, NY: Harper and Row, 1985).
3. Neil Anderson and Steve Russo, *Seduction of Our Children* (Eugene, OR: Harvest House Publishers, 1991).
4. Wendell Amstutz, *Exposing and Confronting Satan and Associates* (Rochester, MN: National Counseling Resource Center, 1992).
5. *Diagnostic and Statistical Manual of Mental Disorders, Fourth Edition (DSM IV),* (Washington, D.C.: American Psychiatric Association, 1994).

AEROMANCY
Divination using observation of air currents as they affect a water surface. (1:521)

AGE OF AQUARIUS
Astrologers believe that evolution goes through cycles directly corresponding to the signs of the zodiac, each lasting approximately 2000 years. Advocates of the New Age say we are now living in the cycle associated with Aquarius. The Aquarian Age will supposedly be characterized by a heightened degree of spiritual or cosmic consciousness. (3:233)

AGORAPHOBIA
An anxiety disorder characterized by anxiety about, or avoidance of, places or situations from which escape might be difficult or in which help may not be available in the event of a panic attack. (5:393)

AKASHIC RECORDS
Assumed vast reservoir of knowledge. Some New Agers believe that the events of all human lives have been recorded in the Universal Mind or Memory of Nature in a region of space known as the ether. (3:233)

ALCHEMY
Often associated with medieval folklore, this is a chemical science and speculative philosophy designed to transform base metals into gold. It is figuratively used regarding the change of base human nature into the divine. (3:233)

ALTERED STATES
States other than normal waking consciousness, such as daydreaming; sleep-dreaming; hypnotic trance; meditative, mystical or drug-induced states; or unconscious states. (3:233)

ANCESTOR WORSHIP
The Chinese practice of honoring or appeasing the spirits of dead relatives. (1:522)

ANOREXIA NERVOSA
An eating disorder characterized by a refusal to maintain a minimally normal body weight and a disturbance in perception of body shape and weight. (5:539)

ANXIETY DISORDERS
Disorders characterized by periods of intense fear and physical discomfort such as shortness of breath, dizziness, sweating and nausea. They include panic disorder with or without agoraphobia, simple phobias, obsessive compulsive disorder and post-traumatic stress disorder. (5:393ff.)

ARITHMANCY
Divination by assigning mystical significance to personal numbers such as a birthday. (1:523)

ASCENDED MASTER
A highly evolved individual who is no longer required to undergo lifetimes on the physical plane in order to achieve spiritual growth. (3:233)

ASTRAL PROJECTION
Sometimes known as "astral travel" or "out of body experience." The spirit or "astral body" appears to be released from the physical body during a trance or altered state of consciousness, resulting in sensations and perceptions of travel. (2:18,19)

ATHEISM
The general belief that there is no God. (1:524)

ATTENTION DEFICIT HYPERACTIVE DISORDER
A disorder characterized by persistent inattention, fidgeting, distractibility, forgetfulness and poor impulse control that is excessive for the age level and evident before the age of 7. (5:78ff)

AURA
An apparent envelope or field of colored radiation said to surround the human body and other animate objects with the color or colors indicating different aspects of physical, psychological and spiritual condition. (3:233)

AUTOMATIC WRITING
A person enters a trance state and appears to write under the control of a spirit. Associated practices are automatic drawing and automatic speaking. (2:21,22)

AURA-READING
Gaining insight into others by interpreting the psychic energy field that supposedly surrounds every living being. (2:21)

BAHAISM
The teaching that all races and religions are in a process of continuing revelation that culminated in the birth of Mirza Husayan Ali or Abdul-Baha in Tehran in 1817. In its view, all religions are different paths to the same God. (2:23)

BAPTISM FOR THE DEAD
The Mormon practice of temple baptisms for dead relatives. (1:525)

BIOFEEDBACK
A technique using instruments to self-monitor normally unconscious involuntary body processes, such as brain waves, heartbeat and muscle tension. As this information is fed to the individual, he or she can consciously and voluntarily control internal biological functions. (3:233)

BIPOLAR DISORDER
Formerly referred to as "manic depression," this mood disorder is characterized by times of intense activity, inflated self-esteem and decreased sleep (manic episodes) and by times of decreased activity, low self-esteem and increased sleep (depressive episodes). (5:350ff)

BLACK MAGIC
Using spells and occult practices for destruction and revenge. It is contrasted with "white magic" which is supposed to be helpful and positive. (1:526)

BLACK MASS
Held in honor of the devil on the witches' Sabbath. The ritual reverses the Roman Catholic mass, desecrating the objects used in worship. Sometimes the participants drink the blood of an animal during the ceremony. Often a nude woman is stretched out on the altar, and the high priest concludes the ritual by having sex with her. (3:239)

BLOOD PACTS
Informal or formal agreements sealed by the parties cutting themselves

and co-mingling their blood, drinking blood or signing a document in blood. (2:31)

Bloody Mary
Teen seance "game" in which participants spin around in a dark room such as a bathroom with their eyes tightly shut, then open them suddenly, and look into a mirror for a scary face to appear. (Source unknown.)

Book of Shadows
Also called a *grimoire*, this journal is kept either by individual witches or Satanists or by a coven to record the activities of the group and the incantations used. (3:239)

Buddhism
A major world religion founded by Siddhartha Gautama who was born in Nepal around 563 B.C. The religion is a path to enlightenment through upward rebirths or reincarnations. (2:24)

Bulimia nervosa
An eating disorder characterized by binge eating usually followed by a purging of the food through self-induced vomiting, the use of laxatives and diuretics, or strict dieting and excessive exercise. There is also a disturbance in the perception of body shape and weight. (5:539)

Capnomancy
Divination using patterns of smoke given off by the fires of offerings or by ritual incense. (2:36)

Cartomancy
Divination using cards, especially Tarot cards. (2:37)

Chakras
The seven energy points on the human body, according to New Agers and yogis. Raising the Kundalini (see definition) through the chakras is the aim of yoga meditation. Enlightenment (Samadhi) is achieved when the Kundalini reaches the "crown chakra" at the top of the head. (3:234)

Chalice
A silver goblet used for blood communions. (3:239)

CHANNELING
A New Age form of mediumship or spiritism. The channeler yields control of his or her perceptual and cognitive capacities to a spiritual entity with the intent of receiving paranormal information. (3:234)

CHILDREN OF GOD
A "Christian" cult founded by David Berg in the late 1960s in California. He became known as David Moses and claims to be the prophet for this generation. He is best known for teaching the use of casual sex to gain converts. The cult is now known as the Family of Love. (2:529)

CHRISTIAN SCIENCE
Religious cult founded by Mary Baker Eddy that teaches the illusion of all matter and evil. Her teachings are contained in the book *Science and Health*, first published in 1875. (2:43)

CHURCH OF JESUS CHRIST OF LATTER DAY SAINTS
Also known as the Mormon Church, this cult was founded by Joseph Smith, Jr. in 1830. Major beliefs include the idea that man can become god. (1:530)

CHURCH OF SATAN
The best known center of open Satanic worship. It was founded by Anton La Vey in San Francisco in 1966. According to Drury, the church ceased to function in 1975 and was replaced by the Temple of Set, headed by Michael Aquino. (1:530, 2:44)

CLAIRAUDIENCE
The ability to hear mentally without using the ears. (3:234)

CLAIRVOYANCE
The ability to see mentally beyond ordinary time and space without using the eyes. Also called second sight. (3:234)

CLAIRVOYANT
One who can see into the spiritual realm in the present, over distance or through time. (1:530, 2:45)

CONSCIOUSNESS
Mental awareness of present knowing. New Agers usually refer to consciousness as the awareness of external objects or facts. (3:234)

CONSCIOUSNESS REVOLUTION
A New Age way of looking at and experiencing life. The primary focus of the new consciousness is oneness with God, all mankind, the earth and the entire universe. (3:234)

COSMIC CONSCIOUSNESS
A spiritual and mystical perception that all the universe is one. To attain cosmic consciousness is to see the universe as God and see God as the universe. (3:234)

COVEN
A group of Satanists or witches who gather to perform rites. There are traditionally 13 members, but with self-styled groups the number varies. A coven is also called a clan. (3:239)

CRYSTALS
New Age advocates believe that crystals contain incredible healing and energizing powers. Crystals are often touted as being able to restore the flow of energy in the human body. (3:234)

CULT
From a Christian perspective, a group that, while claiming to be "Christian," denies at least one major tenet of historical Christian doctrine. In a non-technical sense, the word applies to any system of religious or magical belief. (1:531, 2:53)

CURSE
Invocation of an oath associated with black magic or sorcery intended to harm or destroy property or opponents. (3:239)

DEFENSE MECHANISM
Automatic psychological process (such as projection, splitting, suppression and denial) that protects the individual against anxiety and prevents awareness of internal or external stressors or dangers. (5:765)

DEISM
The belief that God exists but does not interact with His creation. (1:532)

DELUSION
A false belief based on incorrect inference about external reality that is firmly sustained despite what almost everyone else believes and despite what constitutes incontrovertible proof or evidence to the contrary. (5:765)

DEMONIZATION
Sometimes called demon possession. The belief that demons can inhabit or in some way control the thoughts and actions of people. (1:532,533)

DEPRESSIVE EPISODES AND DISORDERS
Recurring and pervasive feelings of fatigue and worthlessness, accompanied by lack of concentration, no interest in pleasure and disturbances in sleep or eating habits. These episodes can be short-lived and mild or can go on for years as in Dysthymic Disorder. (5:320ff)

DHARMA
Law, truth or teaching used to express the central teachings of the Hindu and Buddhist religions. Dharma implies that essential truth can be stated about the way things are and that people should comply with that norm. (3:234)

DISSOCIATIVE DISORDERS
Any of a number of disorders including Dissociative Amnesia, Dissociative Fugue, Dissociative Identity Disorder (formerly Multiple Personality Disorder) and Depersonalization Disorder in which there is a marked disturbance or alteration in the normal integrated functions of consciousness, memory, identity or perception of the environment. (5:477)

DIVINATION
Methods of discovering the personal, human significance of present or future events. The means used to obtain insights may include dreams, hunches, involuntary body actions, mediumistic possession, consulting the dead, observing the behavior of animals and birds, tossing coins, casting lots and reading natural phenomena. (3:234)

DIVINE LIGHT MISSION
Guru Maharaji Ji claims to have eight million followers in this cult of meditation. (2:65)

DOWSING OR DIVINING
The use of a "v"-shaped rod to find underground water or minerals. (1:534)

DRUIDS
A branch of dangerous and powerful Celtic priests from pre-Christian Britain and Gaul who are still active today. They worship the sun and believe in the immortality of the soul and reincarnation. They are also skilled in medicine and astronomy. (3:239)

DUNGEONS AND DRAGONS
Also called simply "D and D," a fantasy role-playing game which uses demonology, witchcraft, voodoo, murder, rape, blasphemy, suicide, assassination, insanity, sex perversion, homosexuality, prostitution, Satan-type rituals, gambling, barbarianism, cannibalism, sadism, desecration, demon summoning, necromantics, divination and many other teachings. (4:409)

EATING DISORDERS
A chronic disturbance of normal eating patterns including Anorexia Nervosa, Bulimia Nervosa and Pica (the eating of non-nutrient substances) (5:539)

ECTOPLASM
A jelly-like substance thought to be left behind by materializations at seances. (2:72)

ECHKANKAR
Known simply as ECK, a group founded in 1964 by Paul Twitchell, who thought himself to be the 971st master in the line of "cosmic current" that flowed through Jesus, St. Paul and others. (2:261)

ESOTERIC
Used to describe knowledge that is possessed or understood by a select few. (3:234)

ESP
Extra-sensory perception. The experience of or response to an external event, object, state or influence without apparent contact through the known senses. ESP may occur without those involved being aware of it. (2:83)

EST
A cult founded by Werner Erhard which emphasizes the realization of one's own deity. (1:535)

EXORCISM
Ceremony at which evil or satanic forces are banished from a location or from a person. (2:82)

FACTIOUS DISORDERS
These disorders are characterized by physical or psychological symptoms that are intentionally produced or feigned in order to assume the sick role. (5:471)

FETISHISM
The worship of a symbolic object talisman regarded as having magical powers. (2:87)

FIRE WALKING
The ability to walk through fire without being harmed usually gained by entering into a trance state. (2:89)

FORTUNE-TELLING
Predicting or guiding the future through divination forms including astrology, Tarot and numerology. (2:93)

FREEMASONRY
Originally an esoteric, occultic society that originated in England in the 14th century. It still has elaborate secret codes and ceremonies, but now has the reputation of a benevolent society. (2:94)

GHOSTS
Believed to be the spirit or "astral body" of a departed person who died and now usually haunts the location where he or she once lived. (2:99)

GNOSTICISM
The secret doctrines and practices of mysticism whereby a person may come to the enlightenment or realization that he or she is of the same essence as God or the Absolute. The Greek word *gnosis* means knowledge. At the heart of Gnostic thought is the idea that revelation of the hidden gnosis frees one from the fragmentary and illusory material world and teaches him or her about the origins of the spiritual world to which the Gnostic belongs by nature. (3:235)

GREAT INVOCATION, THE
A New Age prayer that has been translated into over 80 languages. The purpose of this prayer is to invoke the presence of the cosmic Christ on earth, thus leading to the oneness and brotherhood of all mankind. (3:235)

HALLOWEEN
The October 31 holiday known in occult circles as "All Hallow's Eve." A pagan religious festival celebrating the transition from fall to winter in which the spirits of departed relatives return. (2:8)

HARE KRISHNAS
Common name for members of the International Society for Krishna Consciousness, a Hindu sect stressing ascetic practices. (1:539)

HARMONIC CONVERGENCE
The assembly of New Age meditators at the same propitious astrological time in different locations to usher in peace on earth and a one-world government. (3:235)

HEX
In witchcraft, a spell or curse inflicted upon a person or property. (2:116)

HIGHER SELF
The most spiritual and knowing part of oneself, said to lie beyond ego, day-to-day personality, and personal consciousness. The higher self can be channeled for wisdom and guidance. Variations include the oversoul, the super-consciousness, the atman, the Christ (or Krishna or Buddha) consciousness and the God within. (3:235)

HINDUISM
A syncretistic and polytheistic religion native to India which includes belief in reincarnation and the transmigration of the soul to an eternal state called "nirvana." (1:540)

HOLOGRAM
A three-dimensional projection resulting from the interaction of laser beams. Scientists have discovered that the image of an entire hologram can be reproduced from any one of its many component parts. New Agers use the hologram to illustrate the oneness of all reality. (3:235)

HOODOO
Form of cult-magic originating in Africa in which charms are worn to bring one good luck or to direct misfortune on an enemy. (2:120)

HOROSCOPE
In astrology, a figure or map of the heavens at a point in time by which an astrologer interprets favorable or unfavorable influences in a person's life. Commonly these predictions are categorized by the signs of the zodiac according to a person's birthday. (2:121)

HUBBARD, L. RON
A science fiction writer who founded the Scientology cult. (1:540)

HUMANISM
The philosophy that upholds the primacy of human beings rather than God or any abstract metaphysical system. Humanism holds that man is the measure of all things. (3:235)

HUMAN POTENTIAL MOVEMENT
A movement with roots in humanistic philosophy that stresses man's essential goodness and unlimited potential. (3:235)

HYPNOTISM
Inducing a trance state in which the subject's subconscious state can be brought to the surface and influenced by the hypnotist or hypnotherapist. (2:124)

HYPOCHONDRIASIS
Persistent fear of or belief that one has serious illness contrary to medical diagnosis. (5:462)

I CHING
A Chinese book of divination dating from at least 1000 B.C. (2:125)

INCUBI AND SUCCUBI
Male and female sexual spirits or demons that are said to visit people at night, subjecting them to sexual lust and nightmares. (2:129)

INITIATION
An occult term generally used in reference to the expansion or transformation of a person's consciousness. An initiate is one whose consciousness has been transformed to perceive inner realities. There are varying degrees of initiation, such as first degree, second degree, etc. (3:235)

INNER SELF
The inner divine nature possessed by human beings. All people are said to possess an inner self, though they may not be aware of it. (3:236)

INTERDEPENDENCE/INTERCONNECTEDNESS
Used by New Agers to describe the oneness and essential unity of everything in the universe. All reality is viewed as interdependent and interconnected. (3:236)

ISLAM
The word means "submission" in Arabic and is the religion founded by Mohammed. The key profession is "there is no God but Allah, and Mohammed is His prophet." (2:132)

JEHOVAH'S WITNESSES
Members of the Watchtower Bible and Tract Society cult founded in 1874. They deny the doctrine of the trinity and the deity of Christ. (1:542)

JIANISM
Indian religion founded by Mahavira, a savior-figure who is but one of 24 "saviors." Followers believe in the concept of karma and avoid harming any creatures, including insects. (2:133)

KARMA
The debt accumulated against the soul as a result of good or bad actions committed during one's life or lives. If one accumulates good karma, he supposedly will be reincarnated to a desirable state. If one accumulates bad karma, he will be reincarnated to a less desirable state. (2:139)

KIRILIAN PHOTOGRAPHY
A photographic process accidentally discovered by Soviet electrician Semyon Kirilian in which a luminous "corona" is photographed by using electrical discharges around a person's body. (2:143)

KORAN
The sacred scripture of Islam containing revelations to Mohammed. (1:545)

KUNDALINI
From a Sanskrit term meaning "coil" or "spiral," this term refers to the spiritual energy that may be aroused by yoga and channeled through chakra points. Kundalini is often represented as a coiled serpent. (1:545)

LAVEY, ANTON SZANDOR
American Satanist who founded the Church of Satan in San Francisco, California, and author of *The Satanist Bible 1969* and *The Satanic Rituals 1972*. (1:545)

LEVITATION
The act of raising the human body or another object without any visible means. (2:151)

LIGHT AS A FEATHER, STIFF AS A BOARD
Teen seance "game" in which participants gather around someone and attempt to levitate them using only the tips of their fingers, usually while chanting in unison, "Light as a feather, stiff as a board." (Source unknown.)

LUCIFER
In astrology or astronomy, the name given to the planet Venus as the morning star. It became one of many names given to the devil, the demonic adversary of God. In the theosophical tradition, Lucifer is thought to be

a personification of the independent and self-conscious mind which desires to evolve toward the "light" through many lifetimes. (2:157)

LYCANTHROPY
The belief that a man can be transformed into a wolf through sorcery. (2:159)

MAGIC
The harnessing of natural and supernatural powers for one's use by means of secret rituals and spells. (2:161)

MAGIC CIRCLE
A circle inscribed on the floor of a temple for ceremonial purposes. Often nine feet in diameter, it is believed to hold magical powers and protect those involved in the ceremony from evil. (3:236)

MAGIC EIGHT BALL
A liquid-filled ball, usually black, with a clear window on the bottom. By shaking the ball and looking through the window on the bottom to the words "Yes," "No," and "Maybe" printed on the sides of a die inside, guidance and insight is sought from spirits. (Source unknown.)

MAGICK
Magic that employs ritual symbols and ceremony, including ceremonial costumes, dramatic invocations to gods, potion incense and mystic sacraments. (3:240)

MAGISTER
The male leader of a coven. (3:240)

MAGUS
A male witch. (3:240)

MANIC-DEPRESSION
See "bipolar disorder."

MANTRA
A holy word, phrase or verse in Hindu or Buddhist meditation techniques. A mantra is usually provided to an initiate by a guru who sup-

posedly holds specific insights regarding the needs of his pupils. The vibrations of the mantra are said to lead the mediator into union with the divine source within. (3:236)

MASONS
See "Freemasonry."

MATERIALIZATION
The alleged ability of mediums to conjure up the dead at a seance in a form in which they can actually be seen. (2:173)

MEDIUM
One who acts as an intermediary between the spirit world and the world of normal reality using a variety of occult techniques. (2:175)

MOHAMMED
The founder of Islam who lived from 570 to 632 A.D. (2:181)

MONISM
Literally means "one." In a spiritual framework, refers to the classical occult philosophy that all is one; all reality may be reduced to a single unifying principle partaking of the same essence and reality. Monism also relates to the belief that there is no ultimate distinction between the creator and the creation. See "pantheism." (3:236)

MOONIES
Followers of Rev. Moon. See "Unification Church."

MORMONS
Common name for the members of the Church of Jesus Christ of Latter Day Saints, a quasi-Christian cult founded by Joseph Smith in 1830. They teach a multiplicity of gods and salvation by works. (1:530)

MOSLEM OR MUSLIM
A devotee of Islam and a follower of Mohammed. (2:183)

MYSTICISM
The belief that God is totally different from anything the human mind can think and must be approached by a mind without content. Spiritual

union or direct communion with ultimate reality can be obtained through subjective experience, such as intuition or a unifying vision. (3:236)

NECROMANCY
A practice in which the spirits of the dead are summoned to provide omens for discovering secrets of past or future events. (2:190)

NECROPHILIA
An act of sexual intercourse with a corpse. (3:240)

NEW AGE MEDICINE
A general term applied to many forms of "spiritual" healing practices that use knowledge of chakras or energy points in the human body. Practices would include acupuncture and acupressure. (4:405,398)

NEW AGE MOVEMENT
The most common name for the growing penetration of Eastern and occultic mysticism into Western culture. The words "New Age" refer to the Aquarian Age which occultists believe is dawning, bringing with it an era of enlightenment and peace. Encompassed within the New Age movement are various cults which emphasize mystic experiences. (3:237)

NIRVANA
Literally, a blowing out or cooling of the fires of existence. It is the main term in Buddhism for the final release from the cycle of birth and death into bliss. (3.237)

NUMEROLOGY
Occult system that attributes symbolic meaning to numerical values assigned to the letters of the alphabet (A=1, B=2, etc.). The analysis of hidden prophetic meanings of numbers. (2:196, 3:237)

OBSESSIVE-COMPULSIVE DISORDER
A pervasive pattern of obsessions (intrusive thoughts or images) and compulsions (hand washing, ordering, checking) that is excessively time consuming, interfering with normal activity. (5:417,418)

OCCULT
From the Latin *occultus*, meaning "secret" or "hidden." The occult refers

to the supernatural, to secret or hidden knowledge available to initiates, and sometimes to paranormal phenomena and parapsychology. (3:240)

OLD RELIGION
Expression used by contemporary wiccan devotees to describe witchcraft. (2:199)

OMEN
A sign related to some future event that may occur spontaneously or through divination. (2:200)

OUIJA BOARD
A board containing numbers, letters and the words "Yes" and "No" upon which seance participants jointly move a pointer in an attempt to receive messages from spirits. (2:203)

OUT-OF-BODY EXPERIENCE (OBE)
An experience characterized by the sensation that one's consciousness is operating separate from one's body. Astral projection or astral travel is the ability to produce the OBE at will or in an altered state. (2:203)

PALMISTRY OR PALM READING
Also called chiromancy, divination by interpreting the location and length of the lines and markings on the palm. (2:43)

PANIC ATTACKS
Discrete times of acute fear characterized by some of the following symptoms: shortness of breath, dizziness, palpitations, trembling, sweating, choking, nausea, numbness, chest pain or fear of dying. (5:393)

PANTHEISM
The belief that God and the world are ultimately identical; all is God. Everything that exists constitutes a unity, and this all-inclusive unity is divine. God is equated with the forces and laws of the universe but is not a personal being. (3:237)

PARADIGM SHIFT
Refers to a shift in worldviews. The so-called new paradigm (new model or form) is pantheistic (all is God) and monistic (all is one). (3:237)

PARAPSYCHOLOGY
General term used to describe the study of paranormal phenomena including mental telepathy, ESP, psychokinesis, and out-of-body experiences. (2:206)

PERSONALITY DISORDERS
An enduring pattern of inner experience and behavior that deviates markedly from the expectations of the individual's culture, is pervasive and inflexible, begins by early adulthood, is stable over time and leads to distress or impairment. *The Diagnostic and Statistical Manual of Mental Disorders* recognizes the following specific personality disorders with their associated characteristics:
- Paranoid—Distrust and suspiciousness of other's motives.
- Schizoid—Detachment from social relationships and limited emotional expression.
- Schizotypal—Acute discomfort in close relationships, distorted perceptions and eccentric behavior.
- Antisocial—Disregard for and the violation of the rights of others.
- Borderline—Instability in relationships, self-image and affectations, and marked impulsivity.
- Histrionic—Excessive emotionality and attention seeking.
- Narcissistic—Grandiosity, need for admiration, lack of empathy.
- Avoidant—Social inhibition, feelings of inadequacy, and hypersensitivity to negative evaluation.
- Dependent—Submissive and clinging behavior related to an excessive need to be taken care of.
- Obsessive-Compulsive—Preoccupation with orderliness, perfectionism and control. (5:629)

PLANETIZATION
New Age advocates believe that the various threats facing the human race require a global solution called planetization. It refers to the unifying of the world into a corporate brotherhood. (3:237)

POLTERGEIST
German word for a noisy, mischievous, destructive spirit (demon). (2:123)

PRECOGNITION
Awareness of future events. (2:214)

PROGNOSTICATION
Another word for fortune telling. (1:553)

PSI
The twenty-third letter of the Greek alphabet. A general New Age term for ESP, psychokinesis, telepathy, clairvoyance, clairaudience, precognition and other paranormal phenomena that are nonphysical in nature. (3:237)

PSYCHIC
A medium, "sensitive," or channeler. Also refers to paranormal events that can't be explained by established physical principles. (3:237)

PSYCHIC BIRTH
A quickening of spiritual or cosmic consciousness and power. This new consciousness recognizes oneness with God and the universe. Psychic birth is an occult counterfeit of the Christian new birth. (3:237)

PSYCHIC SURGERY
Healing techniques in which the practitioners claim that the force of God opens bodies and removes diseased organs or tissue without medical instruments. Has been proven to be a hoax in most cases. (2:217)

PSYCHOKINESIS (PK)
The power of the mind to influence matter or move objects. See "telekinesis." (3:237)

PSYCHOMETRY
Using a present object such as a watch, ring, etc. to determine personal characteristics of its owner who is not present. (2:217)

PSYCHOTIC
A term used to describe a variety of symptoms such as delusions, hallucinations, disorganized speech and behavior. (5:273)

PYROMANCY
Divination by interpreting the color and shape of flames in a ritual fire. (2:218)

REINCARNATION
The belief that the soul moves from one bodily existence to another until, usually after many lives, it is released from historical existence and absorbed into the Absolute. (3:238)

RHAPSODAMANCY
A form of divination in which one opens a sacred book and gives special significance to the first line that one sees. (2:225)

RIGHT-BRAIN LEARNING
The right hemisphere of the brain is believed to be the center of intuitive and creative thought (as opposed to the rational nature of the left hemisphere). New Agers have seized on this as a justification to bring right-brain learning techniques into the classroom. These techniques include meditation, yoga and guided imagery. (3:238)

RITUAL
A prescribed form of religious or magical ceremony. (3:240)

ROSICRUCIANISM
Name popular among occult groups that claims inspiration from the 17th century mystic Christian Rosenkreuz which promotes and participates in a variety of occultic practices. (1:356)

RUNES
A northern European alphabet used by occult groups in secret writing. There are several forms of runes. (3:240)

SANTERIA
A mingling of African tribal religions and Catholicism established by African slaves brought to the Americas and the Caribbean. (3:240)

SATANISM
The practice of worshiping Satan often through the mocking of Christian ritual such as the mass. (2:231)

SCIENCE OF CREATIVE INTELLIGENCE
See "TM."

SCIENTOLOGY
Cult founded by science fiction writer L. Ron Hubbard. It is a mix of psychology, occultism and science fiction. (1:558)

SCHIZOPHRENIA
A psychotic disorder characterized by some of the following symptoms: delusions, hallucinations, disorganized thinking and behavior, catatonic behavior, or flat affectation. (5:274ff)

SEANCE
A gathering of people seeking communication with deceased loved ones or famous historical figures through a medium. (2:233)

SEER
One who prophesies concerning the future or "sees" future events. (2:234)

SELF-REALIZATION
A synonym for "God-realization." It refers to a personal recognition of one's divinity. (3:238)

SET
In Egyptian mythology, Set is the dark god, the personification of evil. (2:236)

SHAMAN
A sorcerer, magician, medicine-man or witch doctor who mediates between people and the spirit realm by entering a trance state at will. (2:236)

SILVA MIND CONTROL
A cult which combines self-hypnosis and pop psychology founded by Jose Silva, a Texas hypnotist. (1:559)

SO MOTE IT BE.
Words spoken at the end of an occult ceremony. Similar to "amen" in traditional religious services. (3:240)

SORCERY
Gaining supernatural powers through magical spells and incantations. (2:242)

SPEAKING IN TRANCE
Also known as a "mediumistic trance" and "automatic speaking." A person in an altered state of consciousness often called a "medium" appears to be controlled by a spiritual entity who speaks through them. The medium often has no recollections of the things said during the trance. (2:258)

SPELL
An incantation in the form of magic words or phrases which contain power for good or evil. (2:243)

SPIRIT GUIDE
A spiritual entity who provides information or guidance often through a medium or channeler. The spirit provides guidance only after the channeler relinquishes his or her perceptual and cognitive capacities into its control. (3:238)

SPIRITISM
The French form of spiritualism associated with Allan Kardec that focuses on reincarnation and contacting the dead. (2:244)

SUCCUBI
See "Incubi."

SWEDENBORGIANISM
Emanuel Swedenborg 1688-1772 was a scientist who wrote religious and mystical books. His followers founded the New Church in 1788. (2:249)

SYNCRETISM
The fusion of different forms of belief or practice; the claim that all religions are one and share the same core teachings. (2:249)

SYNERGY
The quality of "whole making": the New Age belief in the cooperation of natural systems to put things together in ever more meaningful patterns. (3:238)

TABLE LIFTING OR TABLE TILTING
Sometimes known as "table turning." Participants usually place their hands palms down with fingers connected in an unbroken circle on top

of a small, wooden table. At times the table appears to quiver, rotate or lift in response to a summoning of spirits. (2:250)

TALISMAN
A power object, usually an amulet or trinket. (3:240)

TANTRA
A series of Hindu or Buddhist scriptures concerned with special yogic practices for swift attainment of enlightenment; also the practices, techniques and traditions of these teachings. (3:238)

TAOISM
Mystical Chinese religion founded by Lao-tzu. (1:562)

TAROT CARDS
A pack of seventy-eight cards commonly used in divination. (2:251)

TEACUP READING
Also called "tasseography." The dregs of a cup of tea are swirled and patterns read as omens of future events. (2:252)

TELEKINESIS
A form of psychokinesis (PK); the apparent movement of stationary objects without the use of known physical force. (3:238)

TELEPATHY
The ability to communicate "mind to mind" without using normal means of communication through the senses. Sometimes called "mental telepathy." It is seen as evidence of "extrasensory perception." (2:252)

THEOSOPHY AND THEOSOPHICAL SOCIETY
A cult founded by Helena P. Blavatsky which mixes heterodoxical Christianity with Hindu theology and spiritist practices. (1:563)

THIRD EYE
An imaginary eye in the forehead believed to be the center of psychic vision. (3:238)

TM
A common abbreviation for transcendental meditation, a Hindu cult imported to the west by Maharishi Mahesh Yogi which focuses on a meditation technique.

Tourette's Disorder
A tic disorder characterized by involuntary motor movements or vocalizations including obscene words. (5:101)

Trance
An altered state of consciousness, induced or spontaneous, that gives access to many ordinarily inhibited capacities of the mind-body system. Trance states are generally self-induced. (3:238)

Unification Church
Quasi-Christian cult founded in Korea and imported to the west by Rev. Sun Myung Moon as the "Lord of the Second Advent." (1:564)

Unitarianism
The belief that God is only one person, denying the deity of Christ and the doctrine of the trinity. (1:564)

Unity School of Christianity
Gnostic cult founded by Charles and Myrtle Fillmore with headquarters near Lee's Summit, Missouri. (1:564)

Visualization
Also known as guided imagery; refers to mind over matter. Visualization is the attempt to bring about change in the material realm by the power of the mind. (3:238)

Voodoo
An ancient religion combining sorcery and Catholicism. Those involved are extremely superstitious and are heavily involved in fetishism. (3:240)

Warlock
Often used for a male witch, but word actually designates a traitor. (3:240)

WATCHTOWER
The periodical of the Jehovah's Witness cult published by the Watchtower Bible and Tract Society. (1:565)

WAY INTERNATIONAL
Quasi-Christian cult founded by Victor Paul Wierwille which denies the deity of Christ. (1:565)

WHITE MAGIC
Magic alleged to be positive, good or helpful by its practitioners. (1:566)

WICCA
Contemporary witches often prefer this Old English title for their practice of witchcraft. The pagan end of the witchcraft spectrum. (1:566)

WITCH
A male or female practitioner of any sort of witchcraft. (3:241)

WITCHCRAFT
Magic, sorcery and occultic practices revolving most often around casting spells and necromancy. A practice of occultic arts, from wiccan nature worship to satanic worship. (1:566, 3:241)

YIN AND YANG
Popular symbols which represent balanced opposites in Chinese thought. (1:567)

YOGA
Literally, yoking or joining. Any system or spiritual discipline by which the practitioner, or yogi, seeks to condition the self at all levels—physical, psychic and spiritual. The goal of the Indian religious tradition is a state of well-being, the loss of self-identity and absorption into the Absolute or Ultimate Being. (3:239)

YOGI
A master of one or more methods of yoga who teaches it to others. (3:239)

ZEN
A type of Buddhist thought best known for its emphasis on breaking

down the commitment and attachment to the logical and rational ordering of experience. (3:239)

ZODIAC
The imaginary belt in the heavens that encompasses the apparent paths of all the principal planets except Pluto. Divided into 12 constellations or signs based on the assumed dates that the sun enters each of these "houses" or symbols, the zodiac is used for predictions in astrology. (3:239)

ZOROASTRIANISM
A religion founded by Zoroaster, born c. 650 B.C., which stresses an eternal battle between good and evil. (1:567)

Help Others Find Freedom in Christ

The **Helping Others Find Freedom in Christ** resources.

Help people become better connected to God using a process called "discipleship counseling." Neil Anderson gives clear guidelines for leading others through the steps to freedom outlined in his best-selling books, **Victory over the Darkness** and **The Bondage Breaker.**

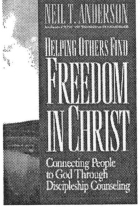

Helping Others Find
Freedom in Christ
By Neil T. Anderson
ISBN 0-8307-1740-4

Helping Others Find
Freedom in Christ
Training Manual & Study Guide
A guide to establishing a
freedom ministry in your church.
Includes an inductive study of
Helping Others Find
Freedom in Christ.

Helping Others Find Freedom in Christ
Training Manual & Study Guide
By Neil T. Anderson and Tom McGee, Jr.
ISBN 0-8307-1759-5

Helping Others Find Freedom in Christ
Video Training Program
A complete program to help you train others to be
part of a freedom in Christ ministry. Includes two
videocassettes, six copies of The Steps to Freedom in
Christ guidebook, one copy of Helping Others Find
Freedom in Christ and one copy of the Helping
Others Find Freedom in Christ Training Manual &
Study Guide.

Helping Others Find Freedom in Christ
Video Training Program
SPCN 8-5116-0094-9

Also available:
The Steps to Freedom in Christ
A step-by-step guide to use in leading someone through the steps to freedom.
Includes a questionnaire and personal inventory as well as instructions.
8.5"x11" guidebook   ISBN 0-8307-1850-8

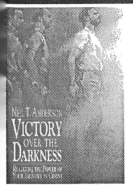

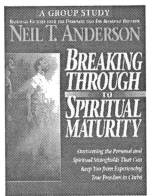

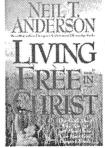

More Resources from Neil Anderson and Freedom in Christ to help you and those you love find freedom in Christ.

Books

Victory Over the Darkness
The Bondage Breaker
Helping Others Find Freedom in Christ
Released from Bondage
Walking in the Light
A Way of Escape
Purity Under Pressure (Youth)
Setting Your Church Free
Living Free in Christ
Daily in Christ
The Seduction of Our Children
Spiritual Warfare
Stomping Out the Darkness (Youth)
The Bondage Breaker Youth Edition
To My Dear Slimeball
Know Light No Fear

Personal Study Guides

Victory Over the Darkness
    Study Guide
The Bondage Breaker
    Study Guide
Stomping Out theDarkness
    Study Guide
The Bondage Breaker Youth Edition
    Study Guide
Extreme Faith
    Youth Devotional

Teaching Study Guides

Breaking Through to Spiritual Maturity
    (Group Study)
Helping Others Find Freedom in Christ
    (Study Guide)
Busting Free
    (Youth Group Study)

Freedom in Christ Conducts Conferences!

Freedom in Christ Ministries is an inter-denominational, international, Bible-teaching church ministry which exists to glorify God by equipping churches and mission groups, enabling them to fulfill their mission of establishing people free in Christ. Thousands have found their freedom in Christ; your group can too! Here are some conferences your community can host which would be led by Freedom in Christ staff:

Freedom for Leaders (a two-day conference of renewal and freedom for leaders).

Living Free in Christ (a seven-day Bible conference on resolving personal and spiritual conflicts).

Spiritual Conflicts and Counseling (a two-day advanced seminar on helping others find freedom in Christ).

Setting Your Church Free (a leadership conference on corporate freedom for churches, ministries, and mission groups).

Breaking the Chains (a young adult conference for college age, singles, and young marrieds).

Stomping Out the Darkness (a youth conference for parents, youth workers, and young people).

Setting Your Youth Free (an advanced seminar for youth pastors, youth workers, and parents).

Purity Under Pressure (a conference for teens on living a life of sexual purity).

The Seduction of Our Children (a seminar for parents and children's workers wanting to lead children to freedom in Christ).

Resolving Spiritual Conflicts and Cross-Cultural Ministry (a conference for leaders, missionaries, and all believers desiring to see the Great Commission fulfilled).

The above conferences are also available on video and audio cassettes. To order these and other resources, write or call us.

To host a conference, write us at:
Freedom in Christ
491 East Lambert Road
La Habra, CA 90631
Phone: 310-691-9128 Fax: 310-691-4035

life. We have been clearly warned: "The Spirit explicitly says that in later times some will fall away from the faith, paying attention to deceitful spirits and doctrines of demons" (1 Timothy 4:1).

By focusing the discussion of Satan's influence on believers on the issue of the location of the demons—whether they are internal or external—some have needlessly polarized the Church. Conservative Christians have disagreed for years about what demons can do to believers and whether this control can extend to what we normally think of as internal functions such as thinking, feeling and motor activities. We could quote authors, cite references and debate the passages, but we don't believe deciding the location is the critical issue. Furthermore, we believe you could use our discipleship-counseling model regardless of your view on the location issue. Let us explain.

First, the issue of internal versus external is hard to apply in the spiritual realm. As believers, is our "skin," the armor of God, repelling demons and their activities? Or is the battle for our minds fought in a spiritual realm where spatial concepts are not the key issues? The indwelling of the Holy Spirit is primarily a "relational issue" and not a "spatial" issue because of the doctrine of the omniprescence of God. The indwelling of the Holy Spirit does not automatically keep sin and evil out of our mortal bodies (study Romans 6-8). The Corinthian believers were warned about receiving other spirits besides the Holy Spirit (see 2 Corinthians 11:3,4) even though Paul calls them temples of the Holy Spirit (see 1 Corinthians 6:19). As the temple of God was violated in the Old Testament, Paul teaches that sin can reign in the mortal bodies of those who use their bodies as instruments of unrighteousness (see Romans 6:12-16). That is why he urges us to present our bodies to God as a living sacrifice (see Romans 12:1) as the necessary prerequisite to the renewing of our minds (see Romans 12:2). The whole question of "internal versus external influence" is difficult because we just don't know exactly how the material world of the brain, body and nervous system interfaces with the spiritual realm of the mind, flesh and spirit.

Second, virtually all who carefully study this issue agree that believers can be greatly impacted by evil spirits. Authors who advocate an external-influence-only view conclude this: "The Bible itself does not give us a full description of everything demons are capable of. Because of this lack of accurate information, plus the satanic ability to deceive, plus our own shortcomings in the area of discernment, it is likely that certain activities such as vocal chord control or even a demon throwing someone on the ground,

(See other side of page.)

Old Man (Col. 3:9)	By Ancestry	New Man (Col. 3:10)
Children of Wrath (Eph. 2:1-3)	By Nature	Partaker of Divine Nature (2 Pet. 1:4)
In the Flesh (Rom. 8:8)	By Birth	In the Spirit (Rom. 8:9)
Walk After the Flesh (Rom. 8:12,13)	By Choice	Walk After the Spirit or After the Flesh (Gal. 5:16)

So is it proper to describe ourselves as "saints who sin" rather than "sinners" if we still struggle with the flesh? Again, popular terminology is a little confusing. "I'm just a sinner saved by grace" has been used at times to express humility before God, and humbling ourselves before God is good. But this phrase has also been used to rationalize the absence of victory over sin, which isn't good.

A quick survey of the Bible yields much strong support for the view that God wants believers to see themselves as saints. In the King James Version, believers are called "saints," "holy ones," or "righteous ones" more than 240 times. In contrast, unbelievers are called "sinners" over 330 times. Clearly, the term "sinner" is normally used to refer to an unbeliever and the term "saint" to a believer. Only three possible exceptions are found—1 Timothy 1:15; James 4:8; James 5:20. Even if all these three uses of the word "sinner" refer to believers, only one could possibly refer to a mature believer's humble perspective of himself as a "sinner" (an interpretation of the use of the present tense in 1 Timothy 1:15 that is open to debate based on the contextual fact that Paul is looking back on his conversion). The passages in James refer either to believers functioning like "sinners" in bondage to sin or to unbelievers who have not yet experienced faith in Christ.

In conclusion, by a ratio of at least 240 to 1, the biblical emphasis is to view ourselves as saints, saved by the grace of God, who still struggle with sin in the flesh. By a ratio of at least 330 to 3, "sinner" would be the normal biblical designation for an unbeliever. In using our material, it doesn't matter if you still prefer to think of believers as having two competing natures (old nature and new nature) as long as your view of our new identity in Christ corresponds to the biblical view of the real power and victory this identity can give us over sin. We think believers will experience greater victory if they trust the biblical view of themselves as saints who are "dead to sin but alive to God in Christ Jesus" and who therefore now